Volume 20

THE COMPLETE ENCYCLOPEDIA OF
CRAFTS

Distributed by Columbia House, 51 West 52nd Street, New York, New York 10019
Printed in U. S. A.

COLUMBIA HOUSE/New York

Contents

Creative Ideas

76/Foam rubber houses. Simple pattern for foam rubber, fabric and glue. **2129**

77/Wind chimes. Creative use of spoons. **2157**

78/Patchwork wall. Decoration the whole family can do. **2185**

✱**79**/Jigsaw puzzles. A coping saw, plywood and favorite pictures. **2213**

Paper

✱**56**/A tissue paper hot air balloon — surprisingly easy to make for a sport which is fun for the family.
Author: Michael Boys. **2130**

57/Decorating with marquetry.
Author: Anita Lear. **2158**

58/Introduction to papier mâché. **2186**

Leather

10/Hot tooling on leather. A belt to make and decorate.
Author: John Williams. **2134**

✱**11**/Carving and modeling.
Author: John Williams. **2208**

12/Handbags from soft leather. A clutch bag to make. **2230**

Front Cover Photograph: Ken Kirkwood
Back Cover Photograph: Peter Dorp

Color /Paint

35/Cleaning oil paintings. Surface cleaning; repairing canvas; varnishing.
Author: Edwina Pickett. **2138**

36/Restoring and painting tinware.
Author: Michael Carmichael. **2218**

Wood / Modeling

10/Carving a wooden bowl. Wood carving tools; suitable woods.
Author: John Matthews. **2142**
(See also Carpentry chapter 18, page 1466.)

Cloth/Sewing

26/How to make a 'papoose carrier'. Pattern of cutting lay-out, step-by-step directions for making.
Author: Anne Johnson. **2146**

Enamel

✱**10**/Cutting shapes for enameling. Using tin snips and a piercing saw building up large items. **2148**

11/The art of 'cloisonné'.
Author: 'Sienna'. **2174**

12/The art of 'champlevé'.
Author: Richard Casey. **2200**

Lapidary

8/More ideas for using slabs.
Author: Denis Inkersole. **2152**

Design Know-how

75/Interior design: window treatment. **2156**

76/Protractors and triangles. **2184**

77/Straight and parallel lines. **2212**

78/Water-based paints. **2240**

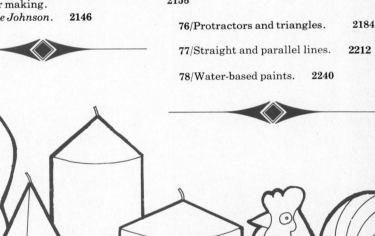

Clay

✻49/A ceramic doll's head.
Author: Anthony Wilson. **2162**
(See also Toys chapter 11, page 2178.)

Yarn/Weaving

25/Spinning with a spindle. How to make a spindle. Teasing and carding wool. Spinning and using the yarn.
Author: Verity Hanson-Smith. **2166**

Wood/Finishes

✻7/Liming, pickling, fuming, scorching.
Author: David Fisher. **2170**

Cloth/Toys

11/How to make a Victorian doll.
Author: Audrey Barker. **2178**
(See also Clay chapter 47, page 2162.)

12/Wardrobe for a Victorian doll.
Author: Audrey Barker. **2196**

Yarn/Macramé

8/Making patterns with Cavandoli.
Authors: Frances Brown and Kit Pyman. **2181**

9/Picture making with macramé. Designing, creating 3-dimensional effects. Choice of knots and background.
Author: Frances Brown and Kit Pyman. **2194**

Flowers and Plants

13/Introducing topiary art.
Author: Graham S. Thomas OBE VMH. **2190**

Home Herbalist

✻5/How to make beeswax polish. Using a solvent; making paste and emulsion polishes; adding carnauba wax. Variations.
Author: Clara Furness. **2204**

Cloth/Patchwork

8/Log cabin patchwork.
Author: Helen Tynan. **2214**

Yarn/Embroidery

18/Colorful modern smocking. Suitable fabrics and preparation; gathering. A choice of decorative embroidery stitches.
Author: Marjory Hastie Smith. **2222**

Shellcraft

1/Introduction to shellcraft. Mollusks and pseudo shells; finding, choosing, cleaning and grading. **2226**

Basketry

19/Introducing corn dollies. An ancient art using straw; cutting, drying, grading and damping. **2234**

Metal

✻31/Ceramic and silver jewelry. Design and step-by-step directions for a necklace. Charms, a silver head, earrings.
Author: Patricia de Menezes.
See also Clay chapter 1, page 5. **2236**

✻ **Not suitable for children without adult supervision**

ADDRESSES
OF MAIL
ORDER SUPPLIERS

ARTS & CRAFTS, GENERAL

California
Gemex Co.
900 W. Los Vallecitos Boulevard
San Marcos, California 92069

Illinois
Lee Wards
Creative Crafts Center
1200 St. Charles Street
Elgin, Illinois 60120

Triarco Arts & Crafts
P. O. Box 106
Northfield, Illinois 60093

Massachusetts
Earth Guild
15 Tudor Street
Cambridge, Massachusetts 02139

Missouri
Skil-Crafts
305 Virginia Avenue
Joplin, Missouri 64801

Nebraska
Mangelsen's
8200 J Street
Omaha, Nebraska 68127

New York
Arthur Brown
2 West 46th Street
New York, New York 10036

Craft Service
337 University Avenue
Rochester, New York 14607

Economy Handicrafts, Inc.
50-21 69th Street
Woodside, N.Y. 11377

Texas
American Handicrafts
P. O. Box 791
Fort Worth, Texas 76101

Wisconsin
Sax Arts and Crafts
207 N. Milwaukee St.
Milwaukee, Wisconsin 53202

BASKETRY

Connecticut
H. H. Perkins
10 S. Bradley Road
Woodbridge, Connecticut 06525

Illinois
Dick Blick Co.
P. O. Box 1267
Galesburg, Illinois 61401

New York
Ace Rattan Products
60-19 54th Place
Maspeth, New York 11378

BATIK

Michigan
Polyproducts Corp.
13810 Nelson Avenue
Detroit, Michigan 48227

New York
Utrecht Linens
33 35th Street
Brooklyn, New York 11232

BEADS

California
The Bead Game
8071 Beverly Boulevard
Los Angeles, California 90048

New York
Grey Owl Indian Mfg. Co., Inc.
150-02 Beaver Road
Jamaica, New York 11433

South Dakota
Del Trading Post
P. O. Box 248
Mission, South Dakota 57555

BOTTLE-CUTTING

New York
Avalon Industries, Inc.
200 Fifth Avenue
New York, New York 10010

CANDLE-MAKING

California
Gemex Co.
900 West Los Vallecitos Boulevard
San Marcos, California 92069

General Supplies Co.
526 Aviation Road
Fallbrook, California 92028

Sippewisset Wax Works
Box 453
Seaside, California 93955

Florida
Island Crafts
5735 14th Street W.
Bradenton, Florida 33507

Illinois
Triarco Arts & Crafts
P. O. Box 106
Northfield, Illinois 60093

Massachusetts
International Candle House
349 Congress Street
Boston, Massachusetts 02210

K.R. Ruckstuhl, Inc.
P. O. Box 663
Provincetown, Massachusetts 02657

Missouri
Skil-Crafts
305 Virginia Avenue
Joplin, Missouri 64801

Nebraska
Mangelsen's
8200 J Street
Omaha, Nebraska 68127

New Jersey
A. I. Root
1106 East Grand Street
Elizabeth, New Jersey 07201

New York
Economy Handicrafts, Inc.
50-21 69th Street
Woodside, N.Y. 11377

Pennsylvania
George Arold
P. O. Box 99
Hatfield, Pennsylvania 19440

Texas
American Handicrafts
P. O. Box 791
Fort Worth, Texas 76101

Washington
Barker Enterprises
15106—10th Avenue S. W.
Seattle, Washington 98166

Pourette Mfg. Co.
6818 Roosevelt Way, N. E.
Seattle, Washington 98115

Wisconsin
Sax Arts and Crafts
207 N. Milwaukee St.
Milwaukee, Wisconsin 53202

CANING AND RUSHING

California
The Caning Shop
1279 Gilman Street
Berkeley, California 94704

Naturalcraft
2199 Bancroft Way
Berkeley, California 94704

Connecticut
H. H. Perkins
10 S. Bradley Road
Woodbridge, Connecticut 06525

Illinois
Dick Blick Co.
P. O. Box 1267
Galesburg, Illinois 61401

New York
Alnap Co., Inc.
66 Reade Street
New York, New York 10007

CERAMICS MATERIALS AND CLAY

Indiana
American Art Clay Co., Inc.
4717 West 16th Street
Indianapolis, Indiana 46222

ADDRESSES
OF MAIL
ORDER SUPPLIERS

JEWELRY FINDINGS AND MATERIALS

California
California Crafts Supply
1419 North Central Park Avenue
Anaheim, California 92802

Gemex Co.
900 W. Los Vallecitos Blvd.
San Marcos, California 92069

Jewelart, Inc.
7753 Densmore Avenue
Van Nuys, California 91406

Illinois
Dick Blick
P. O. Box 1267
Galesburg, Illinois 61401

Triarco Arts & Crafts
P. O. Box 106
Northfield, Illinois 60093

Maryland
CCM Arts and Crafts, Inc.
9520 Baltimore Avenue
College Park, Maryland 20740

Michigan
C. R. Hill Co.
35 W. Grand River Avenue
Detroit, Michigan 48226

New York
Allcraft Tool & Supply Co., Inc.
22 West 48th Street
New York, New York 10020

Economy Handicrafts, Inc.
50-21 69th Street
Woodside, N.Y. 11377

Magic Novelty Co., Inc.
95 Morton Street
New York, New York 10014

Vanguard Crafts Inc.
2915 Avenue J
Brooklyn, N.Y. 11210

Ohio
Kraft Korner
5864 Mayfield Road
Cleveland, Ohio 44124

National Artcrafts Supply Co.
12217 Euclid Avenue
Cleveland, Ohio 44160

Wisconsin
Nasco House of Crafts
901 Janesville Avenue
Ft. Atkinson, Wisconsin 53538

Sax Arts and Crafts
207 N. Milwaukee Street
Milwaukee, Wisconsin 53202

KNOTTING AND WEAVING

New Jersey
Boin Arts and Crafts
91 Morris Street
Morristown, New Jersey 07960

New York
P. C. Herwig Co., Inc.
264 Clinton Street
Brooklyn, New York 11201

LEATHERCRAFT

California
California Crafts Supply
1096 North Main Street
Orange, California 92667

Connecticut
S & S Art and Crafts
Colchester, Connecticut 06415

Illinois
Triarco Arts & Crafts
P. O. Box 106
Northfield, Illinois 60093

Massachusetts
Berman Leather
147 S Street
Boston, Massachusetts 02111

Missouri
The Brown Leather Co.
305 Virginia Avenue
Joplin, Missouri 64801

Skil-Crafts
305 Virginia Avenue
Joplin, Missouri 64801

New York
Art Handicrafts Co.
3512 Flatlands Avenue
Brooklyn, New York 11234

Economy Handicrafts, Inc.
50-21 69th Street
Woodside, N.Y. 11377

P. C. Herwig Co., Inc.
264 Clinton Street
Brooklyn, New York 11201

Leathercrafters Supply Co.
25 Great Jones Street
New York, New York 10012

Tandy Leather Co.
330 Fifth Avenue
New York, New York 10018

Wisconsin
Sax Arts and Crafts
207 North Milwaukee Street
Milwaukee, Wisconsin 53202

METALCRAFTING

Illinois
Apollo Metals, Inc.
6650 Oak Park Avenue
Chicago, Illinois 60638

Maryland
CCM Arts and Crafts, Inc.
9520 Baltimore Avenue
College Park, Maryland 20740

New York
Allcraft Tool & Supply Co.
215 Park Avenue
Hicksville, New York 11801

MOSAICS

Illinois
Dick Blick
P. O. Box 1267
Galesburg, Illinois 61401

New York
Economy Handicrafts, Inc.
50-21 69th Street
Woodside, N.Y. 11377

Soriano Ceramics
2021 Steinway Street
Long Island City, New York 11106

NEEDLECRAFTS

California
Gemex Co.
900 W. Los Vallecitos Boulevard
San Marcos, California 92069

Naturalcraft
2199 Bancroft Way
Berkeley, California 94704

Illinois
Lee Wards
1200 St. Charles Street
Elgin, Illinois 60120

New York
Bell Yarn
75 Essex Street
New York, New York 10002

Economy Handicrafts, Inc.
50-21 69th Street
Woodside, N.Y. 11377

Goldman's Yarn Stores, Inc.
4417 13th Avenue
Brooklyn, New York 11219

Alice Maynard
724 Fifth Avenue
New York, New York 10019

Texas
Merribee Needlecraft Co.
2904 W. Lancaster
Ft. Worth, Texas 76107

PAPERCRAFTS AND PAPIER-MÂCHÉ

Connecticut
S & S Art and Crafts
Colchester, Connecticut 06415

Illinois
Dick Blick
P. O. Box 1267
Galesburg, Illinois 61401

ADDRESSES
OF MAIL
ORDER SUPPLIERS

New York
Long Island Ceramic Center
1190 Route 109
Lindenhurst, New York 11757

DECOUPAGE

Illinois
Dick Blick
P. O. Box 1267
Galesburg, Illinois 61401

Missouri
Skil-Crafts
305 Virginia Avenue
Joplin, Missouri 64801

New York
Economy Handicrafts, Inc.
50-21 69th Street
Woodside, N.Y. 11377

Texas
American Handicrafts
P. O. Box 791
Fort Worth, Texas 76101

DYES

Alabama
Owl and Olive Weavers
704 29th Street South
Birmingham, Alabama 35233

California
The Mercantile
P. O. Box 343
Berkeley, California 94701

Kansas
The Yarn Barn
Box 334
730 Massachusetts
Lawrence, Kansas 66044

Massachusetts
Earth Guild/Grateful Union
15 Tudor Street
Cambridge, Massachusetts 02139

Minnesota
The Yarnery
1648 Grand Avenue
St. Paul, Minnesota 55105

New Mexico
Village Wools Fibercraft Materials
and Supplies
308 San Felipe, N. W.
Albuquerque, New Mexico 87104

Oregon
Wildflower Fibers
211 N. W. Davis Street
Portland, Oregon 97209

Pennsylvania
Lenos Handicrafts
2037 Walnut Street
Philadelphia, Pennsylvania 19103

Texas
Craft Industries
1513 West Alabama
Houston, Texas 77006

Utah
Intertwine
217 Trolley Square
Salt Lake City, Utah 84102

ENAMELS AND
ENAMELLING MATERIALS

California
Seaire
17909 South Hobart Boulevard
Gardena, California 90248

Illinois
Thomas C. Thompson Co.
Highland Park, Illinois 60035

Missouri
Skil-Crafts
305 Virginia Avenue
Joplin, Missouri 64801

New York
Allcraft Tool & Supply Co.
215 Park Avenue
Hicksville, New York 11801

Economy Handicrafts, Inc.
50-21 69th Street
Woodside, N.Y. 11377

Texas
American Handicrafts
P. O. Box 791
Fort Worth, Texas 76101

FLOWER-MAKING
MATERIALS

New York
S. Beckenstein, Inc.
130 Orchard Street
New York, New York 10022

GLASS (STAINED)

Arizona
Art Glass of Arizona, Inc.
2047 North 16th Street
Phoenix, Arizona 85006

California
Augustine Glass Works
929-B Pico Boulevard
Santa Monica, California 90405

Glass by Humber
700 Filbert Street
San Francisco, California 94133

Nervo Art Stained Glass Works
4911 Telegraph Avenue
Oakland, California 94609

Illinois
Acme Glass Co.
2215 West Roosevelt Road
Chicago, Illinois 60608

Maryland
CCM Arts and Crafts, Inc.
9520 Baltimore Avenue
College Park, Maryland 20740

Massachusetts
Stained Glass of Hanover
Box 3065
Hanover, Massachusetts 02339

Whittemore-Durgin Glass Co.
Box 2065 AB
Hanover, Massachusetts 02339

Whittemore-Durgin Glass Co.
825 Market Street
Rockland, Massachusetts 02370

New Jersey
Glass Work Bench
159 Main Street
Flemington, New Jersey 08822

Stancraft
2005 Highway 35
Oakhurst, New Jersey 07755

New York
Allcraft Tool & Supply Co.
215 Park Avenue
Hicksville, New York 11801

S. A. Bendheim Co., Inc.
122 Hudson Street
New York, New York 10013

Economy Handicrafts, Inc.
50-21 69th Street
Woodside, N.Y. 11377

Glass Masters Guild
52 Carmine Street
New York, New York 10014

Ohio
Franklin Art Glass Studios
222 East Sycamore Street
Columbus, Ohio 43206

Pennsylvania
Willet Stained Glass Studios
10 E. Moreland Avenue
Philadelphia, Pennsylvania 19118

Texas
American Handicrafts
P. O. Box 791
Fort Worth, Texas 76101

Virginia
Arts & Crafts Studio
7221 Little River Turnpike
Annandale, Virginia 22003

Washington
Alpha Faceting Supply
Box 2133, Dept. C
Bremerton, Washington 98310

Stained Glass Studio
12519 Lake City Way N. E.
Seattle, Washington 98125

ADDRESSES OF MAIL ORDER SUPPLIERS

Triarco Arts & Crafts
P. O. Box 106
Northfield, Illinois 60093

Maryland
CCM Arts & Crafts, Inc.
9520 Baltimore Avenue
College Park, Maryland 20740

Missouri
Skil-Crafts
305 Virginia Avenue
Joplin, Missouri 64801

New York
Economy Handicrafts, Inc.
50-21 69th Street
Woodside, N.Y. 11377

Wisconsin
Nasco House of Crafts
901 Janesville Avenue
Ft. Atkinson, Wisconsin 53538

Sax Arts and Crafts
207 N. Milwaukee Street
Milwaukee, Wisconsin 53202

PLASTICS
California
Cadillac Plastic & Chemical Co.
11255 Vanowen
North Hollywood, California 91605

Georgia
Cadillac Plastic & Chemical Co.
1500 Carroll Drive, N. W.
Atlanta, Georgia 30318

Illinois
Cadillac Plastic & Chemical Co.
1245 West Fulton
Chicago, Illinois 60607

Maine
Soule Glass and Paint Co.
127 Marginal Way
Portland, Maine 04101

Maryland
CCM Arts & Crafts, Inc.
9520 Baltimore Avenue
College Park, Maryland 20740

Massachusetts
Cadillac Plastic & Chemical Co.
269 McGarth Highway
Boston, Massachusetts 02143

Michigan
Cadillac Plastic & Chemical Co.
15111 Second Avenue
Detroit, Michigan 48203

Polyproducts Corp.
13810 Nelson Avenue
Detroit, Michigan 48227

New Jersey
Cadillac Plastic & Chemical Co.
6025 Colonial Highway
Pennsauken, New Jersey 08109

Smooth-On Corp.
1000 Valley Road
Gillette, New Jersey 07933

New York
Cadillac Plastic & Chemical Co.
35-21 Vernon Boulevard
Long Island City, New York 11106

Industrial Plastic
309 Canal Street
New York, New York 10013

The Plastics Factory
119 Avenue D
New York, New York 10009

Ohio
Cadillac Plastic & Chemical Co.
3818 Red Bank Road
Cincinnati, Ohio 45227

Texas
Cadillac Plastic & Chemical Co.
2546 Irving Boulevard
Dallas, Texas 75207

ROCK POLISHING
California
Great Western Equipment Co.
3444 Main Street
Chula Vista, California 92011

New Jersey
Craftools Inc.
1 Industrial Road
Wood Ridge, New Jersey 07075

Ohio
National Artcraft Supply Co.
12217 Euclid Avenue
Cleveland, Ohio 44160

Wisconsin
Sax Arts and Crafts
207 N. Milwaukee Street
Milwaukee, Wisconsin 53202

SILKSCREEN
New York
Arthur Brown, Inc.
2 West 46th Street
New York, New York 10036

STONE GRINDING
California
Felker Manufacturing Co.
1900-F So. Crenshaw Boulevard
Torrance, California 90501

Walter E. Johansen
P. O. Box 907
Morgan Hill, California 95037

Indiana
Gemstone Shop
17561 State Road 23 N. E.
South Bend, Indiana 46635

Texas
Gem Center, U.S.A.
4100 Alameda
El Paso, Texas 79905

WIRECRAFTING
Illinois
Dick Blick
P. O. Box 1267
Galesburg, Illinois 61401

Maryland
CCM Arts & Crafts, Inc.
9520 Baltimore Avenue
College Park, Maryland 20740

Missouri
Skil-Crafts
305 Virginia Avenue
Joplin, Missouri 64801

New York
Allcraft Tool and Supply Co.
215 Park Avenue
Hicksville, New York 11801

Economy Handicrafts, Inc.
50-21 69th Street
Woodside, N.Y. 11377

WOODFINDINGS
Maine
Saunders Brothers
Westbrook, Maine 04092

New York
Duplex Novelty Co.
315 West 35th Street
New York, New York 10001

YARN
California
The Yarn Depot, Inc.
545 Sutter Street
San Francisco, California 94102

Connecticut
Cottage Crafts
Pomfret Center, Connecticut 06259

Minnesota
The Yarnery
1648 Grand Avenue
St. Paul, Minnesota 55105

New York
Economy Handicrafts, Inc.
50-21 69th Street
Woodside, N.Y. 11377

Home Yarn Co.
1849 Coney Island Avenue
Brooklyn, New York 11230

Paternayan Bros., Inc.
312 E. 95 Street
New York, New York 10028

Ohio
Colonial Woolen Mills, Inc.
6501 Barberton Avenue
Cleveland, Ohio 44102

Oregon
Oregon Worsted Co.
8300 S. E. McLaughlin Boulevard
Portland, Oregon 97202

Pennsylvania
Walter McCook & Son, Inc.
31 No. 10th Street
Philadelphia, Pennsylvania 19107

Creative ideas 76

Foam houses

Half the fun of making a foam house is deciding what to make it look like—perhaps a cottage or a town house.

The instructions here are for the yellow and blue house—the walls of which measure 30.5cm x 45.5cm (12"x 18"). The roof is made separately and is 23.4cm (9⅜") high. However, if you already have a block of foam of a different size, adapt the measurements and shape of the design as necessary.

You will need:

2 pieces of plastic foam for house base and roof (cut according to measurements in fig.1).

Light-weight fabric in two colors to cover base and roof plus 1.5cm (⅝") seam allowance on all sides.

Assorted scraps of felt.

General-purpose adhesive, scissors.

To make the base. Following fig.1 cut out six base pieces from fabric.

From felt cut out a door, windows, steps and other details, as appropriate. Apply glue and stick shapes onto base fabric.

With right sides facing sew together house base, leaving three adjacent seams on one side open.

Trim seams. Turn base right side out and insert foam cube.

Overcast final three seams.

To make the roof. Following fig.1 cut out five roof pieces from contrasting fabric.

With right sides facing, sew roof pieces together—leaving three adjacent seams on one side open.

Trim seams. Turn right side out and insert foam.

Overcast final three seams.

Above: a variety of foam houses—each displaying a different style.

1. *Calculate amount of fabric from the size and shape of the foam.*

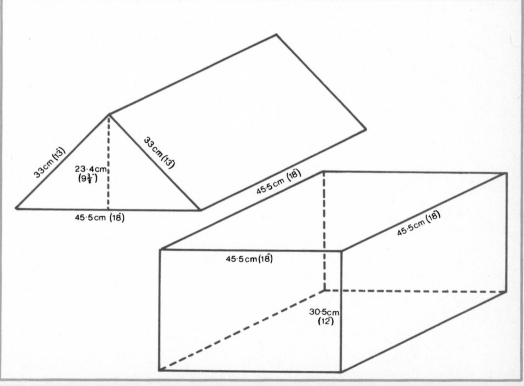

33cm (13) 23.4cm (9¾") 33cm (13) 45.5cm (18) 45.5cm (18) 45.5cm (18) 30.5cm (12)

Liz Whiting

Trevor Lawrence

A tissue paper hot air balloon

In this age of supersonic flight and space travel, it is fun to rediscover the simple pleasure of hot air ballooning. The popularity of ballooning as a sport has greatly increased in recent years, partly because it is an achievement to make something fly in a sustained manner, and partly because making a giant balloon at home is surprisingly easy. It requires only basic materials, mainly tissue paper.

Michael Boys

The principle of ballooning has been known for centuries but it was first demonstrated in France in 1783, by the Montgolfier brothers, who exploited to the full the lifting properties of hot air (which weighs less than cold air and therefore rises).

The distance a balloon travels will depend on the strength of the breeze and whether or not it meets an obstacle, but the type of balloon described in this chapter has been known to travel more than 10 miles. By following a balloon by automobile or on foot you can discover a new sport—the balloon chase—and if you see where the balloon lands (which it will once all the hot air inside has dispersed) you can retrieve it and, with luck, use it for another flight. Fly it out in the open away from trees to make it last longer. When several home-made balloons are entered in a chase and the landing point of each is marked on a map of the local area, a competition can be held for the balloon flying the greatest distance. Balloons made of tissue paper have been known to fly for nearly an hour.

With a little imagination, balloons can be made with different designs, using tissue paper with related or contrasting colors, or by making up each panel in a geometric pattern, as with the 'saw tooth' design shown on page 2133.

A calm day and an open space from which to launch the balloon are essential requirements for this sport. A summer day in the country would be an ideal time and place.

To make a balloon

The following directions are for a balloon about 3m (9') high and just over 1m (3') in diameter in a simple paneled design. It will take two people about two hours to make. It is very important, when gluing, to make sure that there are no gaps or bare spots between the glued edges. Glue should be applied to a depth of 1.5cm ($\frac{1}{2}$") from all edges.

You will need:

48 sheets of colored tissue paper, each measuring about 50cm x 71cm (20" x 28").

A good commercial clear general-purpose adhesive.

Wire about 1mm in diameter (18-19 gauge) and at least 3m (9') long. This will form a ring round the 'neck' of the balloon, to hold it open.

Very fine wire such as fuse wire. This should be cut into two lengths, each about 2m (6') long, to form the neck cross-piece, and there should be enough left over for wrapping round several cotton balls (soaked in denatured alcohol and used as fuel).

A pair of pliers.

Scissors and pencil.

Four large paper clips, bulldog clips or clothes pegs.

A piece of string about 30cm (1') long, to tie round the top of the balloon.

An electric fan heater to test-launch the balloon.

Cotton pads and denatured alcohol for long, fueled flights.

☐ Begin by gluing the shorter sides of four sheets of tissue paper end to end, overlapping each one by about 1.5cm ($\frac{1}{2}$"). Repeat the process with the remaining 44 sheets, making a total of 12 long strips 50cm (20") wide, each using four sheets of paper.

☐ Fold all these strips in half lengthwise and place them on top of one another in a pile, clipping all the

Left: gripped by the wired edge of its neck, the balloon slowly inflates as it is filled with hot air.

Below: the balloon is made from strips of colored tissue paper cut into 'fish' shapes and glued together.

folded edges together with paper or bulldog clips or clothes pegs.

☐ With the pencil, draw a half 'fish' shape on the top folded strip (fig.1) and cut through all the sheets at the same time, following the 'fish' outline. Set aside the tissue paper outside the fish outline but do not discard it.

☐ Keeping the clips or clothes pegs in position, place the folded fish shapes on a flat surface with the straight (folded) edges away from you.

☐ Fold back the top half of the first fish shape.

☐ Stick the next two curved edges together (the top two half fish shapes facing you) along the dotted lines indicated in fig.2. Fold these glued sheets back over the first half fish shape.

☐ Stick the next two curved edges together in the same way and fold them back, repeating the process until there is only one half-fish shape left facing you. Remove the clips or clothes pegs.

☐ Turn all the stuck edges so that the seams are towards the inside. The balloon will then have a smooth curved surface (fig.3).

☐ Apply glue to the two unstuck edges remaining and stick them together. This last seam lies on the outside of the balloon (see fig.3). To strengthen and flatten this seam, apply glue along one side of the seam and gently press it down on to the balloon's surface.

☐ With the help of another person, very gently pull out the sections (from the outside) until the balloon is completely unfurled.

☐ Check for tears in the tissue paper and for gaps in the glued seams. These can be repaired with cellophane or Scotch® tape.

☐ Although all the curved edges have been glued all the way along, you will probably find that there is a small gap in the top of the balloon. Close it by tying a piece of string tightly round the top of the balloon (fig.4).

☐ Make a circle of the thicker wire to fit the neck of the balloon, binding the ends together with Scotch tape. Glue the wire round the inside of the neck, turning under the edge of the tissue paper to form a 'hem' with the wire inside (fig.5). Apply glue to the edge of the paper and stick it down over the wire, to the outer layer of paper.

☐ Finally, make a cross-piece for the neck with two lengths of fine wire, by placing them across the diameter of the thicker wire, so that they cross each other at right angles in the center of the balloon's base (fig.6). Attach to the balloon with Scotch tape.

☐ Test the balloon, indoors if possible, to make sure there are no remaining tears and that it inflates properly. Turn on the fan heater so that it blows hot air into the balloon.

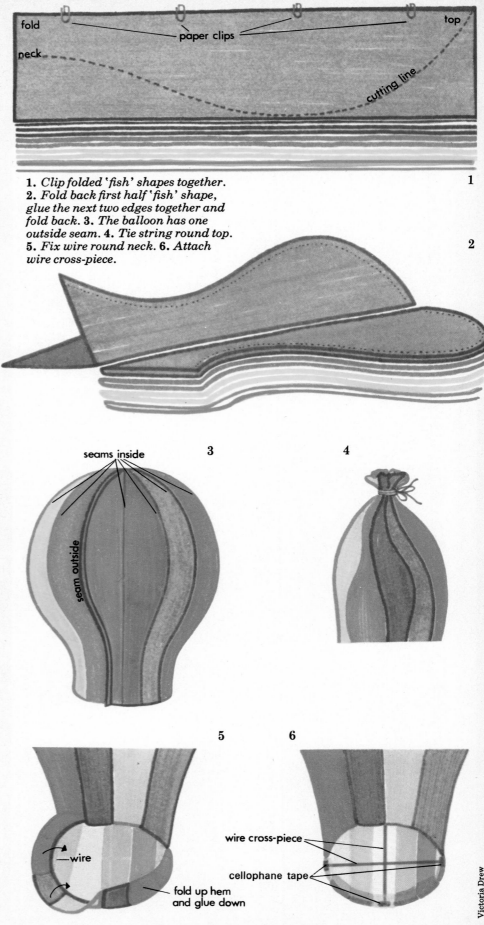

1. *Clip folded 'fish' shapes together.*
2. *Fold back first half 'fish' shape, glue the next two edges together and fold back.* 3. *The balloon has one outside seam.* 4. *Tie string round top.* 5. *Fix wire round neck.* 6. *Attach wire cross-piece.*

Victoria Drew

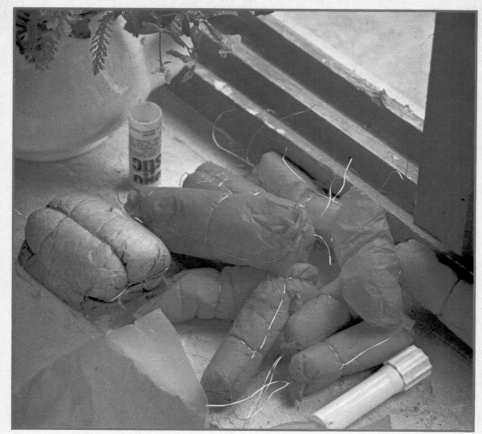

Cotton fuel balls are wrapped in tissue paper and tied with wire.

The beautiful 'saw tooth' balloon in flight. Note the fuel ball burning on the wire cross-piece.

Above: choose a calm day and an open space in which to launch the balloon.

Below: preparing to launch a balloon with the heat from a blowtorch.

Launching

In order to launch and fly the balloon, it must be inflated with hot air. It will fly satisfactorily if it is filled with hot air from an electric fan heater but this is virtually impossible unless you partially inflate it indoors before taking it outside. A blowtorch may also be used for the initial inflation, or the balloon can be inflated by holding it over a small dish in which cotton soaked in denatured alcohol is burning. However, great care must be taken with the last two methods, particularly if children are present.

As the balloon starts to rise, you can fix to the center of the wire cross-piece a ball of absorbent cotton soaked in a small amount of denatured alcohol. To hold the cotton pad together, wrap some of the remaining tissue paper around it and secure with a length of fuse wire, as in the photograph, leaving one end of the fuse wire long enough to attach to the cross-piece. About two tablespoons of denatured alcohol are enough for a fist-sized piece of cotton. A larger piece of absorbent cotton with proportionately more denatured alcohol will result in a longer flight but it will also increase the risk of fire.

Light the absorbent cotton just before releasing the balloon and watch it rise up and away into the air.

2133

Hot tooling on leather

The technique of hot tooling is very similar to the technique of cold tooling explained in the previous leather chapter, but here the tools are used heated. This technique is traditionally used in bookbinding to decorate leather book covers, but it can also be used to make very attractive patterns on many other leather articles.

The results obtained are similar to those of cold tooling, but because the decorative stamps are not struck with a mallet, the impressions are flatter than those made by cold tooling. The heat of the tool makes the leather turn a dark brown color. This causes subtle variations in the color when the leather is dyed.

The leather used for hot tooling is the same as for cold tooling—vegetable-tanned cowhide which has not been given a cellulose or lacquered finish. It is sometimes called 'tooling leather'.

The hide is either used dry or moistened with water for this technique.

The tools are basically the same as those used for cold tooling—the decorative stamps and the tools for drawing single or double lines—but the decorative stamps used for hot tooling are bookbinder's finishing or hand tools made of brass with wooden handles. The tools must be brass so that they will not be damaged during heating. Bookbinder's finishing tools are available in many floral and other motifs which can be used individually or to make up repeat patterns to cover large areas. It is also possible to buy these stamps in letters of the alphabet and numerals. Many motifs are available in wheels that can be run over the leather to produce a continuous line of pattern.

These tools can be bought from specialist bookbinding tools suppliers, and are often chosen from a catalogue and made to order rather than readily available. They are expensive, and only worth buying if you intend to do a lot of this type of work. The same tools used for drawing lines in the previous chapter are also used for hot tooling.

The designs for hot tooling will probably be less varied than for cold tooling as, owing to the cost, the number of stamps you have may be limited. However, it is still possible to make numerous designs using one stamp combined with the single or double lines made by the dividers or edge creaser (see fig.1).

The same principle of design applies as for cold tooling, ie try to make the design look as if it fits in with the shape of the object.

If you want to make a repeat pattern with a stamp, measure the height and width of the stamp and check to see that it will fit an exact number of times into the space allowed in your design.

Making the design. The leather is usually tooled before stitching (to make handling easier) but after cutting and skiving, if necessary.

The design is first drawn to scale on a piece of paper, placed over the leather

A selection of brass bookbinder's finishing tools showing some of the many designs available.

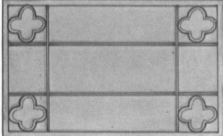

1. *Two designs from one stamp.*

and drawn over to lightly mark the design onto the leather. It can then be tooled.

The tools are heated by holding in a flame or resting on an electric burner. First test the tool on a damp rag which should produce only a slight hiss, and then on a scrap of leather to make sure that it is not too hot. The amount of time the tool will take to heat up depends on the size of the brass stamp—less than a minute should be long enough for most average-sized stamps.

The heated tools can be used on dry or damp leather. The single and double lines can be made quite successfully on dry leather, but a better result will be obtained with the decorative stamps if the leather is moistened first. More care must be taken with moist leather as it will scorch more easily than dry.

When pressed on damp leather, the tool should cause the leather to go brown, but not too dark. If it goes a very dark brown it means that the tool is too hot; if very pale brown, the tool is not hot enough. The piece of leather used for testing should be taken, if possible, from the same hide as you are using for the article, as the amount of heat necessary varies from hide to hide.

When the right color is obtained on the scrap of leather, use the tool on the design. It will be necessary to reheat an average-sized tool after three or four impressions. Always test for heat on the rag and scrap of leather. You will soon get to know how long the tool must be held in the flame or rested on the electric burner in order to obtain the correct degree of heat.

Dyeing. Because hot tooling can only be done on the pale cream-colored leather, it must be dyed after being tooled. This is done as described in the previous chapter.

On the belt (see photograph) the tooled impressions are painted in a variety of colors to emphasize the design.

The belt

The belt is decorated with a 10cm (4″) repeat pattern using hot and cold tooling, and is then dyed and polished. It measures 3cm (1¼″) wide and 92.5cm (36″) long and will fit a waist of up to 80cm (31″).

You will need:
Tools
Sharp craft knife.
Compass with adjustable screw.
Skiving knife.
Diamond stitching awl.
Harness needles.
Stitching clams or vise.
Edge shaver or medium grade sandpaper.

The decoration and colored dyes transform a simple belt into something very special. Designed by John Williams.

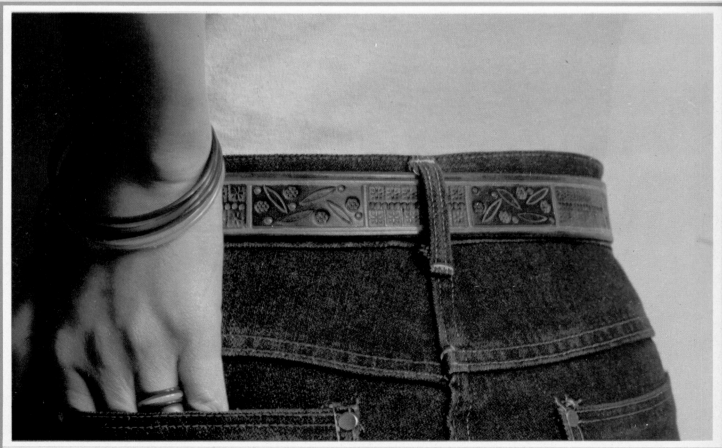

Fine grade sandpaper.
Dividers.
Edge creaser or bone folder.
Rotary punch.
Soft pencil.
Steel ruler.
Piece of hardboard 91cm square (3′ square).
Gas or electric burner.
Bookbinder's finishing tool of your choice. On the belt shown here, three different tools are used, but one will be sufficient to make a pleasing design for a belt.
Steel stamp (or stamps) of your choice for cold tooling, and mallet.
Sable brushes of various sizes.
Felt pad on a wire.
Polishing rags and brushes.

Materials
4mm ($\frac{3}{16}''$) thick vegetable-tanned tooling leather: a strap 3cm ($1\frac{1}{4}''$) wide and 1m (39″) long, and a small piece for the belt loop 9cm ($3\frac{3}{4}''$) long, 1.3cm ($\frac{1}{2}''$) wide.
Linen thread.
Beeswax.
Brass buckle 3cm ($1\frac{1}{4}''$) inside width.
Leather dyes in various colors. If you buy aniline spirit dye you will also need a bottle of the solvent specified on the packet.
Neutral leather polish such as shoe polish.
Leather adhesive.

☐ Make up the belt following instructions in Leather chapter 6, page 1966.
☐ Stitch the buckle with two parallel lines of stitching instead of the V-shape used previously (fig.2).
☐ Do not stitch the loop until the design has been made on it.
Marking the design. Before making any tooled decoration on the leather, the edges of the design should first be marked out.
☐ Set the compass to 3mm ($\frac{1}{8}''$) and scribe a line along each long edge of the belt on the grain side, up to 8cm ($3\frac{1}{4}''$) from the buckle end, and along each long edge of the loop.
☐ The lines on the buckle end of the belt can be marked lightly with a pencil and triangle, and for the other end draw a semi-circle to join up the two lines (fig.3).
☐ Draw lines on the grain side on either side of the lines of stitching, about 2mm ($\frac{1}{16}''$) away from them.
☐ Draw lines across the belt, between the scribed lines to divide it into the panels for the repeat pattern (see fig.3). On the belt shown here, lines are drawn across the belt at intervals of 5cm (2″). This is because the bookbinder's tool used fits an exact number of times into this measurement, allowing for the double line.
☐ Using your bookbinder's tool, check to see which measurement would be

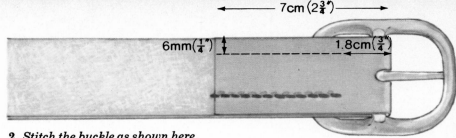

2. *Stitch the buckle as shown here.*

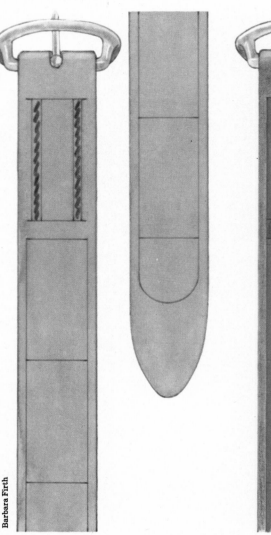

Barbara Firth

3. *The outline of the design is marked around the edge of the belt; lines are drawn to divide it into panels.*

most suitable for your belt and add on about 2mm ($\frac{1}{16}''$) for the double line between the panels (fig.4) which will be made later.
The basic outline of the design has now been marked out.
Decorating the belt. Using the scribed and penciled lines as a guide, the decoration can now be tooled on the belt (see fig.4.)
Before making any marks on the belt, practice the techniques described earlier on a scrap of leather.

4. *The panels on the belt are decorated with hot and cold tooling and dyed various colors.*

First of all, the single scribed and penciled lines are turned into double lines by means of the dividers used in the previous leather chapter on cold tooling.
☐ Heat the dividers over the flame or burner and test to see that they are hot enough.
☐ Following fig.4 run the heated dividers over the line around the edge of the belt and belt loop, turning the single line into a double line. The second line should be inside the first.

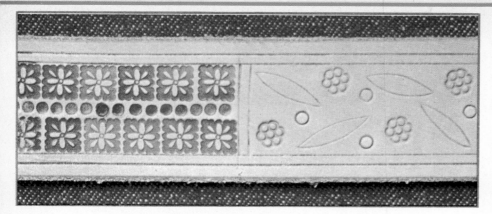

Above: a section of the belt after it has been tooled, ready for dyeing.
Below: the belt section is painted with aniline dyes of various colors.

Melvin Grey

the shank of the tool will remain hot and help to reheat the tool for the next impression.

When applying the tool to the leather, hold it upright in your right hand (if you are right-handed) with your thumb resting on the top of the wooden handle. The upper part of your body should lean well over your work. If you lean over the tool, the pressure will come from your body rather than just your wrist. The larger the face of the tool, the more pressure is needed to make the impression.

The lower part of the tool should be guided onto the leather very carefully and pressed down. A tool with a large face will require a slight rocking motion from side to side and from top to bottom to make a clear impression.

☐ Make the decorations with the bookbinder's tool (or tools) in alternate panels all down the belt.

The other panels can be decorated as you choose, using techniques for hot or cold tooling (or both) as explained in this and the previous chapter. On the belt shown here these panels are cold tooled with decorative stamps—a flower and a dot—and with leaf shapes 'drawn' on the leather with a bone folder.

☐ To avoid monotony, vary the arrangement of these motifs.

☐ Apply the decoration to the buckle end of the belt—on the belt shown here a row of flowers is stamped between the double lines (see fig.4.)

☐ Leave the belt to dry.

Dyeing the belt. The tooled decoration can now be painted with dyes.

☐ Mix up the powder dyes with the solvent specified by the manufacturer in the proportions specified on the package or use the liquid dyes straight from the bottle.

☐ Paint the dyes on the belt and belt loop using small sable brushes for detail and a piece of felt on a wire handle for large areas.

On the belt shown here the back of the belt and the outside edges are dyed brown, the panels using the bookbinder's tool green, the inside of the double line red, and the other panels have a blue background, maroon flowers, green leaves and red dots.

☐ If there are any patches where the dye has not 'taken', rub these with fine grade sandpaper and paint on some more dye. Wait until dry then polish with a canvas rag.

☐ Stitch the belt loop (see Leather chapter 6).

☐ Polish the edges of the belt and belt loop with a damp canvas rag and leave overnight to dry out completely.

☐ Apply a coat of wax polish to the finished belt and give a final polish with a soft brush to remove wax from the tooled impressions.

To obtain a straight line, run the dividers along the edge of the steel ruler.

☐ When you have made double lines around the edge of the belt, make double lines dividing the panels, keeping the second line on the side away from the buckle to keep each panel the right size.

☐ Double the lines on either side of the stitching.

All the lines have now been tooled onto the belt and the panels can now be decorated.

☐ Dampen alternate panels on the belt by painting water on them with a sable brush.

The panels are ready to tool when the color of the leather starts to fade.

☐ Heat the bookbinder's finishing tool over the flame and then test the heat on a rag and scrap of leather as before. If you use a damp rag to cool down the end of the tool to the right temperature,

Cleaning oil paintings

The cleaning of oil paintings in its fullest sense consists of the removal of accumulated dirt and old varnish which have obscured the original work of the artist. The removal of the varnish is not practical for amateurs as strong solvents are necessary and it is very easy to remove the actual painting along with the varnish, ruining the entire work. However, surface cleaning, which does not remove varnish, can be very rewarding, adding new life to an old darkened painting.

Sometimes it is possible to buy old, attractive but dirty oil paintings for very small amounts, or perhaps you even have some rather gloomy relics hung or stored about the house. After making sure that they are of no great value, it can be quite simple to clean them, restoring the colors to their original hues and luster. Whether the oil painting is on wood, hardboard or canvas all you need to do is to remove the accumulated dirt. Watercolors, pastels and gouaches should never be cleaned by amateurs. Consult a professional picture-restorer.

Surface cleaning

Surface cleaning will remove the grime which has accumulated on the top layer of varnish without removing or attacking the varnish or risking any damage to the paintwork itself. Surprising results are often obtained by surface cleaning, provided you never get carried away with enthusiasm and attack the picture too hard.

Before starting, you must carefully examine the picture to make sure that there are no loose particles of paint, flaking, blisters or severe cracking of the paint. If any signs of these are present do not attempt to clean the picture, it will need an expert's attention.

You will need:
Wood or hardboard.
Thin cardboard.
A clean soft brush or cloth.
Round hog hair brush (optional).
Good quality absorbent cotton.
Mineral spirits (turpentine substitute).
Picture cleaner.
Note: you can make your own cleaner but this will be somewhat less effective than the commercial product. A simple recipe is—two parts lemon juice to one part water, or substitute vinegar for the lemon juice.

☐ Carefully remove the picture from its frame and place it on a flat table in a good light.

☐ If the painting is on canvas you will see that this canvas is stretched over a narrow surrounding wooden frame called 'the stretcher'. This leaves the canvas unsupported in the center so you will need to prepare a wood or hardboard 'block' to remedy this (you will need several layers of hardboard to equal the depth of the stretcher) otherwise any pressure would crack the painting over the inner edge of the stretcher (fig.1).

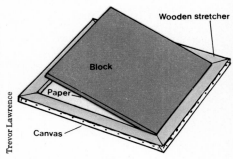

Wooden stretcher
Block
Paper
Canvas
Trevor Lawrence

1. *A block supports the canvas.*

The block should be of the thickness of the stretcher and of the size of the stretcher's interior. You should, in addition, slide pieces of cardboard or layers of paper between the back of the canvas and the stretcher (see fig.1). Do not force in too much cardboard as this will stretch the canvas. The support must be smooth with no lines or bulges as these would show on the cleaned painting's surface and damage the picture.

If the picture has been painted on wood or hardboard there is no stretcher so no support is needed.

☐ Next dust the surface of the painting with a clean soft brush or cloth.

☐ Then with a swab of cotton dipped in mineral spirits wipe gently over the whole painting a few times, replacing the absorbent cotton each time it becomes dirty. You will find that

New life can be given to old pictures once the surface has been cleaned.

Junk shops abound with dark, grimy but rather interesting oil paintings. These can be bought for very little and are fun and rewarding to clean.

cleaner evenly distributed and never allow it to remain in pools on the picture.

☐ When no more dirt is brought off by the cotton swabs, thoroughly wipe the whole picture with fresh swabs, this time moistened with mineral spirits in order to remove completely all traces of cleaner. It is most important that you pass fresh swabs of the spirits over repeatedly in order to take off every vestige of the cleaner as, if any should remain, it may give a white misty effect when dry. If this occurs, further wiping with mineral spirits is necessary.

☐ The picture should now be left to stand for a few hours in a warm, dry, dust-free room before varnishing.

Repairing canvas

The beginner may undertake the repair of small holes and tears in the canvas of an oil painting provided they are not too complicated.

You will need:
A razor blade and a pair of small sharp scissors.

Notice the contrast between the clean, bright, right-hand side of the picture and gloomy left. Leave the cleaning of valuable paintings to experts.

already quite a lot of dirt will have come away and you are able to examine the painting far more clearly.

☐ Stir or shake the cleaning fluid until it is well mixed. Moisten a swab of the cotton with the solution. (If your oil painting has a thick encrusted surface called an 'impasto' it is better to use the round hog hair paintbrush to apply the picture cleaner as strands of cotton could easily pull off or damage the prickly surface of the paint.)

The cleaner should be shaken each time it is used.

☐ Select a corner of the painting of about 3cm sq (1in sq) in an unimportant area of the work, and gently apply the moistened swab with a circular movement. Never press hard or rub vigorously and if any color comes away on your cotton swab, or any unexpected changes occur, discontinue all cleaning and take the picture to an expert.

☐ If no color comes away and no changes occur, you may then proceed to clean the entire picture with a gentle, circular motion. Regularly replace the dirty swabs of cotton (or wipe your brush clean), always shake the cleaner bottle and always check your swabs to see that there is no color of paint on them. Keep the

A small quantity of strong clean white or neutral-colored linen or canvas.

A latex-based adhesive such as is used on fabrics.

A packet of gesso powder (available at most art supply shops).

Retouching varnish (available at most art supply shops).

A pointed hog hair oil paintbrush in one of the finer sizes.

Rag or old cloth.

Artist's oil paints, a tube of each of the following colors: flake white, ivory, black, vandyke brown, vermilion, cobalt blue, cadmium yellow and phthalocyanine green. With these you can mix any shade you require.

☐ First carefully trim away any hanging or broken strands of canvas from the hole or tear at the front of the picture. Do this with either a razor blade or small sharp scissors.

☐ Turn the painting face down on a table. Cut a patch or strip of linen sufficient to cover the tear or hole, allowing a 12mm ($\frac{1}{2}$") margin all around. If you are repairing a tear, you should first bring the broken edges as closely in place as possible before fixing the linen strip behind.

☐ Carefully fix the patch or strip in place at the back of the canvas with a little adhesive. Hold firmly in place with your finger for a few minutes until the adhesive begins to dry. To prevent the edges of the tear wrinkling before it is dry, it may be necessary to weight the patch from the back of the picture with a flat, heavy weight until the adhesive is dry.

☐ Leave the weighted mend to dry out completely for about four hours.

☐ When dry mix in a saucer a small quantity of gesso powder with cold water to form a stiff paste.

Turn the canvas face upward (back on to the support) and with a finger, gently fill in the hole or tear with the gesso paste until it is up to the level of the surface of the painting. Try not to smear the surrounding area with the gesso paste. Leave to dry for at least 24 hours.

☐ Then, with a damp cloth, remove the surplus gesso from the repair and surrounding area, finally smoothing off the surface with the damp cloth. Allow to dry.

☐ Cover the gesso paste area with a little retouching varnish on your finger. Allow to dry for 12 hours.

☐ You may now fill in the area with the exact shade of matching oil color using a fine brush. (Practice mixing your colors on a saucer and try them out on a scrap of linen until the exact shade is obtained.)

After retouching your picture you should leave it to stand for about four weeks before varnishing, so that the small area of fresh color is able to dry out completely.

Varnishing

Varnish protects the painting and brings out the colors and, penerally speaking, a glossy finish is more suitable for older, classical paintings, whereas the matt varnish is often better for modern works.

You will need:

Gloss finish picture varnish or matt picture varnish. A good quality 3cm or 4cm ($1\frac{1}{2}$" or 2") wide hog bristle brush (according to size of picture).

☐ Varnish the oil painting on a flat table in a dry, warm, dust-free room. Dust the painting before applying the varnish. If the varnish is cloudy, the bottle should be left to stand in a bowl of hot water for a few minutes until the fluid becomes clear.

☐ Pour a sufficient quantity of varnish for the whole painting into a saucer.

With the brush, apply the varnish quickly and smoothly with long even strokes right across the painting from side to side; never dab or use short strokes.

Apply sufficient varnish to cover the painting but do not take too much varnish on your brush. The varnish layer must completely cover the picture but at the same time must not be thick. The whole picture should be covered as evenly and quickly as possible. Make sure that every part is covered by observing the surface from an angle against the light. Try to avoid covering the same area twice and make sure that no stray hairs are left on the surface (hence the reason for using a good quality brush). If there are stray hairs lift them off with a pair of tweezers.

☐ Leave to dry for 24 hours in a flat position in the same warm, dry, dust-free room.

☐ When dry, the picture may be refitted into its frame and re-hung. You should be careful to avoid putting fingerprints on the surface of the picture when placing it in its frame as the varnish surface may still be tacky.

Warning: providing the instructions are carried out carefully, no problems should arise, but every picture is different and there is always an element of risk in the cleaning of any painting.

Once the surface of the picture is clean it should be varnished. The varnish not only protects the painting but also accentuates the colors.

Carving a wooden bowl

The craft of wood carving adds new dimensions to the work of the carpenter who makes an effort to learn the skill. Most of the previous modeling chapters specify the use of rasps to shape the wood. However, the abstract sculpture (Modeling chapter 9, page 1998) introduces the firmer gouge, a carving tool used mainly for simple hollowing-out work.

This chapter extends your woodcarving skill by showing you how to go about carving a simple bowl. The tools and types of wood commonly used in carving are also dealt with.

Wood carving tools

Some wood carving processes can be carried out using ordinary bevel edged wood chisels (fig.1). However, more complicated work requires the use of proper wood carving gouges, a selection of which is shown in fig.2.

Professional wood carvers often own over a hundred different gouges to handle all the intricacies of their work; but beginners can start with two or three gouges and add to their kit as the need arises or as your budget permits.

The shafts (or blades) of wood carving tools are classified in three ways: shape (ie straight, curved or bent); width (measured at the cutting edge) and section (ie the shape at the cutting edge).

Straight tools are used mainly for low relief work and for shallow bowls. They can be used for sculpting in the round if the blade is held at an angle of about 15 degrees to the wood.

A variation of the straight carving tool is the spade tool which has a tapered shaft. There are three types of spade tools: the fish-tail or short taper, the medium taper and the long spade.

For carving deeper recesses, such as deep bowls, where it is impossible to use the straight gouge, a curved or long bent gouge can be used or the bent or spoon bit gouge.

Two other types of carving tool are the fluter or veiner tool and the parting or V-gauge. The fluter has a U-shaped section and the V-tool is as the name suggests. The section of the V-gauge comes in three different angles: 45°, 60° and 90°.

Many of the carving processes are done with both hands on the tool—one hand pushing on the handle, the other on the blade, acting as a guide. For much deeper cuts, a carver's mallet is used to drive the tool into the wood. Consequently, clamps and vises are needed to hold the work. An engineer's vise with its padded jaws is very useful for sculpture in the round because it stands above the bench and allows the carver to work right around the object.

Suitable woods

Most wood can be carved though certain types are more suitable than others. Those most suitable are close-grained hardwoods such as beech, sycamore, mahogany, teak or oak. Beech and sycamore are particularly suited for tableware because of the smooth polished finish which can be obtained. The others are used mainly for furniture. Teak, because of the odor it gives off, is unsuitable for tableware.

Softwoods, though easy to carve, are prone to splitting and warping. If you

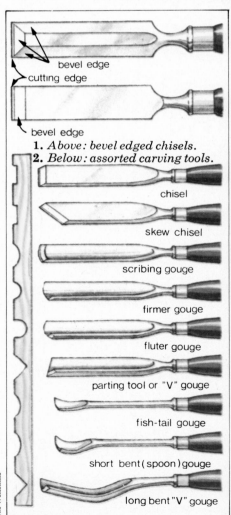

1. *Above: bevel edged chisels.*
2. *Below: assorted carving tools.*

bevel edge
cutting edge
bevel edge

chisel
skew chisel
scribing gouge
firmer gouge
fluter gouge
parting tool or "V" gouge
fish-tail gouge
short bent (spoon) gouge
long bent "V" gouge

Paul Williams

do use them, make sure they have been well seasoned beforehand.

Choose a hardwood that has a uniform texture and a close, even grain.

The bowl

The pear-shaped bowl is about 14cm (5½″) wide, 25mm (1″) deep and 29cm (11½″) long. It is made from hardwood, using the basic principles of carving. As with the abstract sculpture in the previous wood modeling chapter, a mallet is used to make deeper cuts into the wood. The work must always be held firmly in clamps or a vise while being carved.

You will need:

A 22mm (⅞″) wide firmer gouge and a carver's mallet and a half-round file.

C-clamps and a bench vise.

A coping saw and a flat rasp.

Pencil or felt-tipped pen, tracing paper and a sheet of carbon paper.

Wax or varnish finish—optional.

Medium and fine-grade sandpaper.

A piece of hardwood, 175mm x 32mm and 35cm long (7″x 1¼″x 14″).

A shallow bowl and dish carved from hardwood. The small bowl is finished with a clear polyurethane varnish and the dish is waxed. Designer: John Matthews.

Steve Bicknell

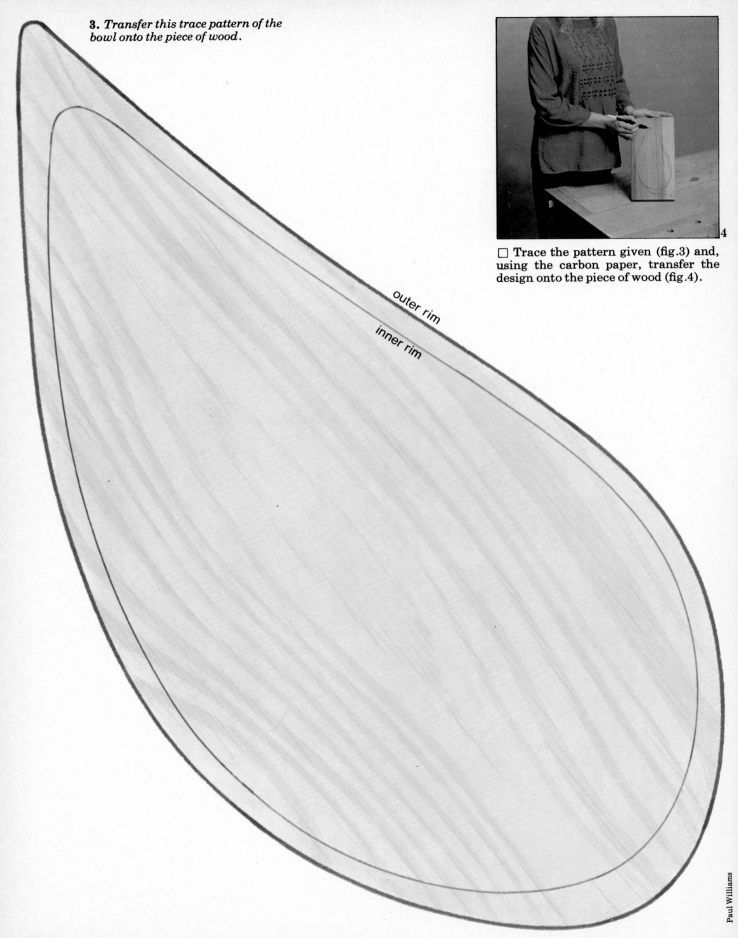

3. *Transfer this trace pattern of the bowl onto the piece of wood.*

outer rim

inner rim

□ Trace the pattern given (fig.3) and, using the carbon paper, transfer the design onto the piece of wood (fig.4).

5

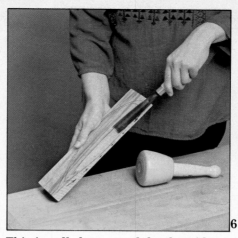
6

7

☐ Fasten the wood to the edge of the table with the C-clamps. Gouge out a channel 25mm (1″) deep along the length of the marked-out bowl (fig.5).

This is called a control depth guide.
☐ This specially prepared cross-section of the bowl (fig.6) shows how the depth guide is set out. Work from

either end of the bowl, gradually getting down to the required depth.
☐ Next, gouge out the waste wood on either side of the depth guide (fig.7).

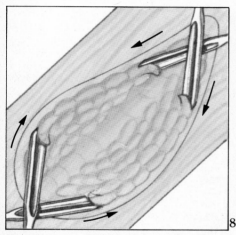
8

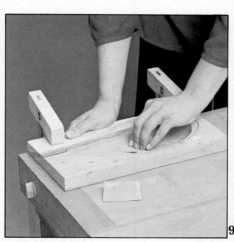
9

10

The diagram (fig.8) shows the directions in which the gouge must be applied at this stage.
☐ When the inside waste of the bowl has been removed, smooth the inside

with medium grade sandpaper and then with fine grade (fig.9). Alternatively, the gouge lines can be left to give the inside of the bowl a 'fluted' finish.

☐ With a coping saw, cut off the outer waste from the sides of the bowl. Cut on the outside of the guide-lines marking the shape of the bowl (fig.10).

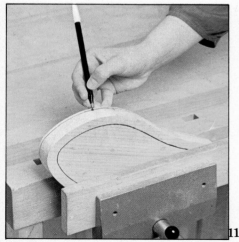
11a

11b

16mm($\frac{5}{8}$″)

base of bowl

3mm($\frac{1}{8}$″)

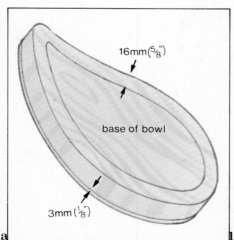

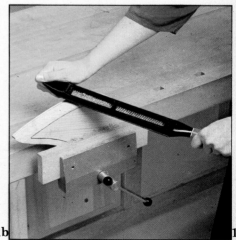
12

☐ Clean down to the lines using a rasp.
☐ With a felt-tipped pen or pencil draw a line 3mm ($\frac{1}{8}$″) from the top of the bowl on the edge. Draw another line

around the base of the bowl, 16mm ($\frac{5}{8}$″) in from the edge (figs.11a and 11b).
☐ With the flat rasp remove the wood between these two lines to make slanted sides (fig.12).

☐ Clean up the wood with a half-round wood file. Smooth, using a medium then fine grade sandpaper.
☐ Apply an appropriate finish. Salad bowls should be rubbed with edible oil.

How to make a papoose carrier

For centuries, women have carried their babies on their backs. Women of the West have, however, viewed this practice with skeptical interest, but recent research has revealed that the gentle swaying movement caused by the mother's walking is in fact soothing and comfortable for the child carried in this way.

Dispense with expensive and awkward baby carriages and make yourself a 'papoose carrier'. It costs a fraction of the price of a carriage, and only takes a few hours to make. It has the added advantage of leaving your hands free. From the moment a baby can support his own head, he can be carried in this manner and there is never any need to worry about leaving your baby unattended.

For the papoose carrier
You will need:
2.8m (3yd) of muslin or any strong cotton fabric, 90cm (36") in width. If you use fabric of a different width, adapt your requirements accordingly by making a cutting layout (see Sewing chapter 8, page 684).
Matching thread.
Ballpoint pen or tailor's chalk.
Scissors.
The straps
☐ Cut two strips of fabric 260cm (102") long by 27cm (11") wide (fig.1).

A papoose carrier is simple and inexpensive to make: rid yourself of the anxiety of parking a carriage, and carry baby the effortless way while he watches the world go by in comfort.

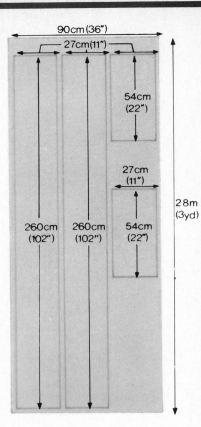

1. *Suggested cutting layout.*

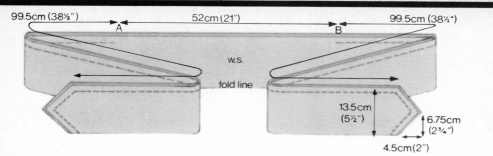

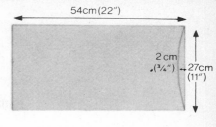

2. *Dimensions of assembled strap, with opening for insertion of central panel.*

3. *Side shaping of central panel.*

☐ Fold them in half lengthwise, right sides facing, and trim the corners to a point as shown in fig.2.

☐ Machine stitch the two halves together, taking a 1cm (⅜″) seam allowance, up to points A and B (see fig.2).

The central panel will be inserted into these openings between points A and B.

☐ Turn the straps right side out and press. Repeat on the other strap.

The central panel

The central panel is made double, as are the straps, for extra strength.

☐ Following the cutting layout, cut two pieces of fabric 54cm (22″) by 27cm (11″).

☐ Place one piece on top of the other, and draw a line freehand with a ball-point pen or tailor's chalk on one of the shorter edges so that it curves in to 2cm (¾″) in the center (fig.3). Fold the two pieces of fabric together in half widthwise and cut along the curved line. In this way, you will obtain a symmetrical curve on each side of both pieces of fabric.

☐ With right sides facing, machine stitch the two pieces of fabric together along the two curved edges, taking 1cm (⅜″) seam allowance.

☐ Turn the panel right side out and press the seamed edges.

☐ Machine stitch again along these two edges on the right side close to the edge. This additional stitching line is for extra strength.

Assembling

☐ Insert 1.5cm (½″) of the two long edges of the central panel into the openings of the straps. Baste in place. Join with two rows of machine stitching, making sure that both rows catch the central panel (fig.4).

How to use the papoose carrier

It is advisable to put the baby into the carrier with the aid of a friend.

☐ Two straps are pulled over the shoulders, and two around the waist, so that the two curved sides of the central panel are on each side of the baby's body.

☐ Tie all four straps together securely, making sure that the waist straps, in particular, are tight.

The gentle movement of walking will rock your baby to sleep.

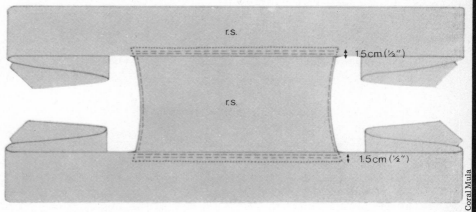

4. *Insert central panel into straps.*

Coral Mula

Cutting shapes for enameling

Using pre-shaped copper blanks for enameling limits designs to the shapes available. It is not difficult, however, to cut shapes from metal, and by making your own blanks the scope for designing is much greater. This chapter covers cutting metal with tin snips and with a jeweler's piercing saw.

In addition, instructions are given for making a rectangular panel by mounting together a series of small cut shapes. This method enables those with small kilns to make large panels.

Using tin snips

The first and easiest way to cut copper is to use a pair of tin snips (jeweler's snips). Tin snips can be used to cut curves and circles but not for more intricate shapes like sharp angles and wavy lines.

You will need:
Equipment. Tin snips.
Mallet with a hide head or a plastic mallet.
Fine-cut hand file (needle files).
Hand drill with metal bit to drill small hole for jump ring (if necessary).
Felt-tipped or ballpoint pen.
Materials. .9mm (19-20 gauge) copper. (For large panels or dishes use 1.25mm (16-18 gauge) or 1.6mm (14-16 gauge).
☐ Mark out the shape required with a felt-tipped pen, close to edge of the copper sheet so as not to waste copper.
☐ Cut out the shape with the tin snips. Use the snips as you would a pair of scissors but do not close the jaws completely—use only the inner area of jaws (fig.1)—the front of the tin snips would make a kink in the metal.
☐ Place the cut-out shape on a hard smooth surface and tap gently with the mallet to flatten it.
☐ With the hand drill and metal bit, drill a small hole to hold a jump ring if it is required.
☐ Smooth the cut edges with needle files.

Using a piercing saw

A jeweler's piercing saw frame and blades are used for more intricate work such as angles and wavy lines and for removing inner sections of a design. It is not, however, difficult to use after a little practice and it cuts quickly through the metal. At first you may

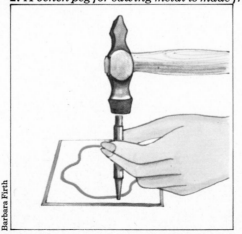

1. *Cutting copper with tin snips.*

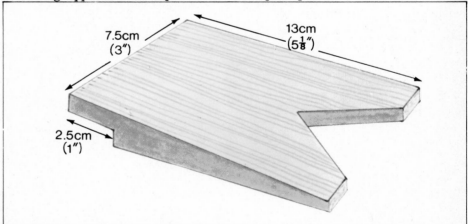

2. *A bench peg for sawing metal is made from a wedge-shaped piece of wood.*

7.5cm (3")   13cm (5⅛")   2.5cm (1")

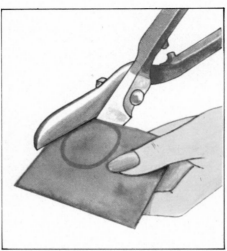

Barbara Firth

3. *Make a mark just off cutting line.*

break the saw blades but you should soon adapt to the rhythm of sawing and the problem will cease.

To insert a blade into the saw frame, clamp one end of the blade into the screw at the end of the frame nearest the handle (the teeth should slope toward the handle). At the same time tighten and tension the other end in position.

You will need:
Equipment. As for cutting with tin snips.
Jeweler's piercing saw frame and blades. (The thinner the metal the finer the blade used, see instructions supplied with saw for correct blade for the thickness you are handling).
Bench peg or board pin (fig.2), available from jeweler's suppliers—or you could improvise using a piece of plywood.
C-clamp. Nail punch (or large nail).
Hammer.
Emery paper.
Paper, scissors and any household glue.
Materials. As for cutting with tin snips.
☐ Secure the bench peg to a steady surface with the C-clamp.
☐ Draw your design on paper with a ballpoint pen.

☐ Cut out the paper into an approximate rectangle, or square, containing the design.
☐ Glue the paper to the copper, with the design uppermost.
☐ Cut the rectangle from the metal using the tin snips. Flatten it by tapping lightly with the mallet.
☐ With the nail punch and hammer, make a mark on the waste area of the copper just off the cutting line (fig.3).
☐ Drill a hole through the mark just large enough for the blade to pass through.
☐ Place the piece of copper, with the design uppermost, on the bench peg. Position the copper so that the cutting is done within the V-shape.

☐ Open one end of the saw, insert the blade through the hole just drilled and then tighten and tension the blade in the frame as previously described.

☐ Hold the metal firmly with one hand and, using the saw with the other, cut along the edge of the design—cutting through the paper at the same time (fig.4). Saw gently with an up-and-down action. Each movement down toward the peg removes a small piece of metal which enables you to follow a line exactly. Do not saw roughly or you will break the blade. If you find it is difficult to saw, increase the tension of the blade little by little until you can control the saw easily.

Stop and adjust the position of the work from time to time, if necessary, to keep the saw blade within the V-shape of the peg and so that the saw can be held comfortably.

☐ To turn a corner continue with the sawing action, but reduce the pressure, and ease the saw gently around so that the cut starts to follow the cover.

☐ When you have cut out a shape, open and remove the saw blade.

☐ Proceed in this way until the whole design has been cut out.

☐ Rub the paper off the copper with emery paper or wash it off.

☐ Use the needle files to smooth all the cut edges and then proceed with enameling in the usual way.

Cutting out a shape within an outline. If your design calls for an area to be cut out inside the basic shape the procedure is slightly different.

☐ When drawing the design on paper, shade all areas to be cut away, ie waste area around edge of design and any inner shape to be cut out.

☐ Glue the paper to the copper, cut out rectangle with tin snips and flatten as previously described.

☐ With the nail punch and hammer make a mark on the waste areas of copper for each cut, ie the shaded portions, just off the cutting line. Drill a hole through each mark for the saw blade to pass through.

☐ Continue as previously described but cut out the shape within the design before going around the outline. If you cut out the outline first you will find it rather awkward to hold the copper firmly when cutting out the inner area.

Building up large items

The size of work which you can enamel is obviously governed by the size of the muffle (firing chamber) of your kiln. This usually limits the home enameler to pieces of jewelry, ashtrays and other small items. One way around the problem of producing larger pieces such as a panel or a teapot stand is to mount together several, separately enameled, squares of copper or irregular shapes which follow the lines of a design

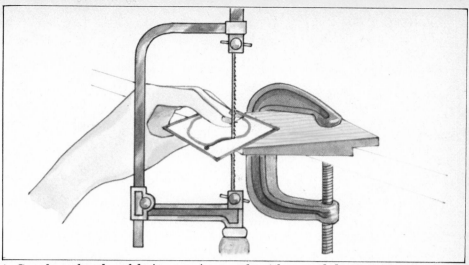

4. *Cut along the edge of design, sawing gently with up-and-down movement.*

Alasdair Ogilvie

Above: branches and leaves in this picture were annealed and shaped before enameling. Designer Phoebe Douglas.

Left: striking 'champlevé' necklace of cut shapes. Designer Esther Austin.

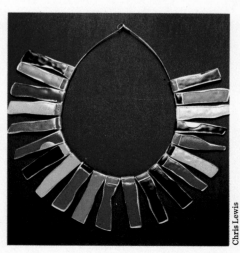

Chris Lewis

rather like the pieces of a stained glass window.

The 'King of Hearts' (shown overleaf) is made following the 'stained glass window' principle, with the component parts of the design mounted onto a piece of wood representing the border of the playing card. The wood can be white as on a real playing card, gold as shown here or any color.

King of Hearts

This project involves several of the techniques covered in previous chapters: using an adhesive, stencils, working with threads and lumps of enamel and painting.

The method of transferring the design to the copper with carbon paper, used for this project, is an alternative to the one described earlier in the chapter. It is a good method to use for simple shapes but not suitable for very intricate cutting.

You will need:

Equipment. See Enamel chapter 1, page 106.

Jeweler's piercing saw and other cutting equipment (except household glue). Wire cutters.

Materials. Wood or hardboard 22.5cm x 15cm (9″ x 6″) painted in the chosen color (for mounting the work).

1.25mm (16-18 gauge) or .9mm (19-20 gauge) copper 17.5cm x 10cm (7″x 4″).

2 small bought heart-shaped copper blanks (or cut your own).

About 15cm (6″) copper wire.

Opaque enamel powders in white, bright yellow, royal blue, scarlet and black.

Transparent deep blue enamel powder (use an opaque enamel if you prefer).

Black painting enamel powder.

Salt and vinegar pickle solution (Enamel chapter 7, page 996).

Anti-fire scale liquid (optional).

Enamel threads in assorted colors.

Small lumps (or chips) of enamel.

Fine paintbrushes.

Tracing paper, fairly hard pencil, carbon paper and drawing pins.

Thin, stiff cardboard.

Scalpel.

Fine file or carborundum stone.

Blowtorch (optional).

Cellulose wallpaper paste with tragacanth base, gum tragacanth or gum arabic.

Brushes for applying pickle, anti-fire-scale liquid and paste.

Strong adhesives.

☐ Switch on the kiln so that it will be hot enough, i.e. bright orange, by the time you are ready to fire.

☐ Take a tracing of the trace pattern (fig.5), including the numbers.

☐ Make sure your piece of copper is completely flat. In its new state the metal is quite shiny and will therefore take neither pencil marks nor carbon marks. To give a mat finish to the copper, brush over it with salt and vinegar pickle. Leave to dry.

☐ When pickle is quite dry, wipe over the copper gently with a clean rag. The surface will now take either pencil or carbon marks.

☐ Lay your piece of copper on a board, place the tracing over it. Keep the tracing in place with thumbtacks at the two top corners just outside the

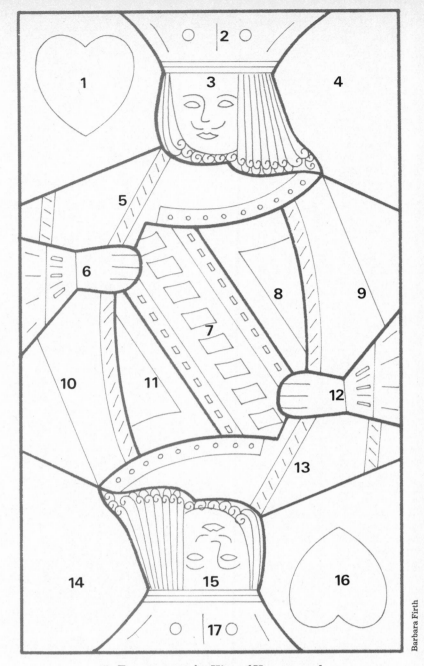

5. Trace pattern for King of Hearts panel.

Barbara Firth

copper. If the tacks are pressed down tightly the heads will keep the copper secure.

☐ Slide a piece of carbon paper under the tracing and draw carefully over the lines to transfer the design onto the metal. Mark in the numbers as well.

☐ Cut out the shapes indicated by the thicker lines (see fig.5). (There is, of course, no need to stick the tracing onto the copper as you have traced out the design with carbon paper.)

☐ As each piece is cut, lay it in its proper place on the tracing. You will notice that as the card looks the same either way up, the shapes are in pairs except for the middle one, number 7. This means you can enamel pieces in

pairs, saving time and electricity.

☐ Prepare pieces 1, 4, 14 and 16 and then give them a coat of white enamel powder. If you wish, give the pieces a thin coat of adhesive before sifting on the powder (Enamel chapter 5, page 514). Many enamelers prefer to use an adhesive rather than sift powder onto a dry piece of copper.

☐ Place pieces singly or in pairs (according to size of kiln) on the wire mesh stand. Dry out if using adhesive, and fire.

☐ Remove loose fire-scale (this must be done after each firing).

☐ Trace a heart shape from fig.5, and with a scalpel, cut a stencil from cardboard (Enamel chapter 4, page 496).

□ Place the heart-shaped stencil in position on pieces 1 and 16 in turn. Paint a thin coat of gum or paste on the heart area and sift on a coat of red enamel powder. Remove stencil carefully (tweezers are useful for this job). Tidy up the edges of the heart shape with a slightly damp, fine brush. Dry piece on top of kiln and then fire.

□ Next, prepare and give the two crowns, numbers 2 and 17, a coat of yellow enamel.

□ Put threads, broken to length, and chips of enamel in place for the decorations, having first sifted on another thin coat of yellow powder to stop them slipping about. (Enamel chapter 6, page 910).

□ Prepare and give the faces, numbers 3 and 15, a coat of white enamel. Then paint in the features and hair carefully with black painting enamel and fire (Enamel chapter 9, page 2080.)

□ Prepare and give numbers 5 and 13 a coat of red enamel, being careful not to over-fire.

□ Break the threads for decoration and have them ready.

□ Cut a shape for each piece in cardboard to mask all but the parts to be

King of Hearts panel—made up in sections, enameled and then mounted on wood. Designer Nigel Goldup.

black and yellow. Shake on these two colors and carefully remove the card. Drop the threads into place using tweezers. Fire.

□ Prepare and give numbers 6 and 12 a coat of white enamel. Have the threads ready.

□ Mask off the hands and shake on deep blue for the sleeves. Place threads with tweezers and fire.

□ Paint in the finger lines and fire in the same way as you did the features. Alternatively, these could be put in with very thin black threads at the same time as the sleeve decoration.

□ Prepare and give numbers 9 and 10 a coat of red enamel. Break threads for decoration. In order to achieve the necessary curve you will have to break the threads into short lengths or bend a thread to shape using a blowtorch (Enamel chapter 6, page 910).

□ Mask off the area on each piece to remain red and shake blue enamel powder over the rest. Remove mask and shake a little red enamel along the

edge where the threads are to be placed. Position the threads carefully with tweezers and fire.

□ Prepare and give numbers 8 and 11 a coat of royal blue enamel. Then mask off the area on each to remain royal blue, give the remaining area a coat of deep blue, in the way previously described, and fire.

□ The center piece, number 7, is the last to be enameled. Have ready the white threads—thin ones for the long stripes and short pieces of thicker thread for the dots.

□ Prepare and give the piece a coat of black enamel.

□ Sift on another very thin layer of black powder, position the threads with tweezers and fire.

□ Cut a stencil for the shapes down the middle of the piece, position it very carefully and shake on red enamel powder. Remove stencil and fire the piece.

□ Clean the backs of all the pieces with emery paper.

□ Clean off the edges of all the pieces with a fine file or Carborundum® stone and then with emery paper in order to insure that they are really bright and smooth. Care in cleaning the edges makes a tremendous difference to the final result.

□ Mark the rectangular shape of the enamel 'card' on the piece of wood with a fine pencil line.

□ Scratch the surface within this area with a sharp point (a nail will do) and scratch the backs of the copper pieces. This gives a key for the glue.

□ Glue the pieces in place on the wood with adhesive.

□ Cover the work with several layers of newspaper and put a heavy weight on top until the glue has set—preferably overnight.

□ The two Ks are made from flattened copper wire. Anneal the wire then place it on a very hard surface (a steel block if you have one) and hammer it to flatten it slightly.

□ Cut with wire cutters into the required lengths. Clean it in the salt and vinegar solution with the two little heart-shaped blanks. Enamel red and fire. Glue in place.

General Hints

Annealing copper. This consists of heating the copper to red heat in the kiln and then plunging it straight into cold water. This serves two purposes: it burns off any grease on the metal and, at the same time, softens it so that it can be easily bent into any shape. The branches and leaves on the enameled wall plaque of a thrush were annealed and bent into shape before enameling.

More ideas for using slabs

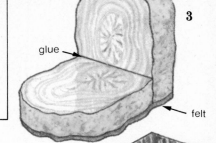

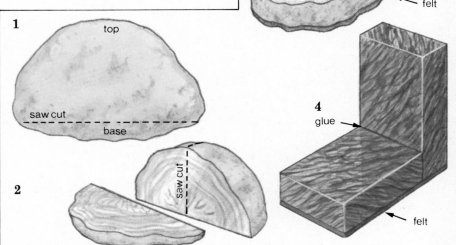

1. *A block of rough for making matching book ends.* 2. *Saw one side of the rough before slicing in half.* 3, 4. *Two ways of making slab book ends.*

Paul Williams

A few projects for using slabs are outlined in Lapidary chapter 6, page 2002. However, if you have the use of a mud saw with a 25-30cm (10-12″) diameter with which you can further shape slabs (as described in Lapidary chapter 7, page 2026), there are many more uses to which such stones can be put.

If making an object from more than one slab, it is important to insure that the slabs you use have patterns which match and blend well together. For example, any banding in the material looks best when it runs in the same direction on all pieces. Matched pairs of slabs can only be obtained from the opposite sides of a single saw cut.

Book ends

There are several ways of making book ends by slabbing roughs. A block of rough such as an agate nodule (a nodule is a stone ball more or less spherical in shape and solid right through) may be sawn in half to form matching book ends.

Colorful banded agate makes a beautiful decoration when sliced at different angles, and book ends are an excellent way to exploit the banded pattern, as the photograph shows. If the base of the rough stone is fairly flat it will just need lapping (see Lapidary chapter 6), but if it has an uneven surface it will be necessary to saw off one side of the stone first, to make a flat base (fig.1). Next, slice off a small piece of rough at right angles to the base (fig.2), before sawing it into two halves. The two sides to be displayed can then be polished to show the matching patterns in the stone.

A book end may also be produced by gluing two slabs (which each have one end trimmed) together at right angles. Use an epoxy resin to join slabs (fig.3). Yet another way is to use two matched slabs for each book end, sawing them into rectangles and lapping their faces and edges. Polish the faces which will be visible (as described in Lapidary chapter 6) and then glue them together with epoxy resin at right angles to each other (fig.4). Glue felt to the base of all types of book ends, to avoid scratching or marking the surface on which they are to be placed.

Matching banded agate book ends made by sawing a block of rough in half.

Kim Sayer

Asprey & Co.

A paper knife

If you own or have the use of a mud
saw, a slab made of a hard material
such as jade, agate or petrified wood
may be trimmed to form a paper-
knife. Fig.5 shows a design for such a
knife with an outline resembling a
rounded spatula or palette knife: the
handle is rounded to an oval cross-
section and the blade portion is ground
to an edge. Fig.6 shows a design with
a pointed blade forming a diamond
shape. You can use either of these
designs or vary them if you wish, but
keep the shape fairly simple and draw
its outline on the flat surface of the
slab with a felt-tipped pen before you
start.

Choose a slab from which you can
make a knife about 15cm (6″) long, 3cm
(1¼″) wide and 4mm ($\frac{3}{16}$″) thick and
make sure that the lines of the pattern
in the stone will travel lengthwise in
the knife. It is less likely to break than
if the lines traveled across it.

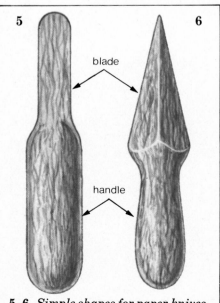

5, 6. *Simple shapes for paper knives.*

*This paper knife from Aspreys, in
London, was designed by Colin Griggs.*

When the slab has been trimmed to the
required shape, remove scratches by
holding the knife in a clamp (the clamp
on your machine if it has one) and
sanding it with silicon carbide paper
glued to a wooden stick with epoxy
resin. Start with coarse paper and
progress to a finer one (see Lapidary
chapter 6, page 2002). Give the knife a
final polish with another wooden stick
around which you've wrapped a piece
of felt dampened with water and
sprinkled with aluminium or cerium
oxide, depending on the stone. Hand
polish the knife vigorously all over
until it shines. Remember that all the
polishing processes will take several
hours of hard work.

Slabs may also be trimmed to form
knife handles, for either a paper knife
or cutlery. The handle must be drilled
to take the shank of the blade.

A box

A very handsome box suitable for holding cigarettes or jewelry can be made from slabs. Choose a fairly soft material such as marble, calcite onyx or alabaster for your first box. You can use slabs of different materials if you wish.

Brass hinges and other fittings such as that on the box shown are readily available from cabinet makers. Hinges may be recessed in the stone, but if they are not, the box lid may be leveled by gluing small felt pads on the opposite side of the lid from the hinges. For a simple, rectangular box with outside measurements of 10cm x 7.5cm x 5cm (4″x 3″x 2″) follow fig.7 for measurements, using slabs which are all 5mm ($\frac{3}{16}$″) thick. The dotted lines indicate the areas to which epoxy resin is applied, on the inside surface of the slabs.

Whatever size and shape of box you choose, the method of construction and number of slabs needed are the same.

You will need:

Five slabs 5mm ($\frac{3}{16}$″) thick for a box without a lid (see fig.7).

Two more thinner slabs if you wish to make a lid, either removable or hinged, one which will be cut to 10cm x 7.5cm (4″x 3″) and about 3mm ($\frac{1}{8}$″) thick and one which will be cut to 9cm x 6.5cm ($3\frac{5}{8}$″x $2\frac{5}{8}$″) and about 1.5mm ($\frac{1}{16}$″) thick after lapping.

Stiff cardboard, cellophane tape, epoxy resin, triangle.

80, 320 and 600 loose grits and lapping plate.

Leather-covered polishing wheel and tin oxide.

Water.

Clamp, rubber bands.

Felt-tipped pen, pencil.

☐ Before cutting and grinding the slabs to their final shape, construct a box from stiff cardboard and tape, numbering all the pieces so that they can be used as templates for drawing the shapes on the slabs. Select the best areas of the slabs for pattern and freedom from flaws, and outline and number shapes with felt-tipped pen.

☐ Begin by trimming slabs around the templates to the correct size.

☐ Lap each side of each slab with a glass lapping plate (or on an electrically driven tin lap if you have the use of one) and coarse (80) grit (see Lapidary chapters 6 and 7) until all saw marks have been removed.

☐ Lap the faces to be on the outside of the box with 320 and 600 grits.

Steve Bicknell

□ Using coarse grit, lap the edges of the base so that all corners are right angles. Check that angles are right angles with the triangle; the base decides the final shape of the box, so it is most important to work accurately.

□ Repeat this lapping process with the edges of the sides of the box, using coarse grit and checking the angles with the triangle. Do not proceed to finer grit as a slightly rough surface enables the glue to adhere to the surfaces more efficiently.

□ Take the base and set side A (see fig.7) against it. Draw a pencil line across the end of this side at the level of the upper face of the base (along the dotted line indicated in fig.7). Do the same with side B, and stick a strip of tape across the bottom of each side, up to the pencil lines.

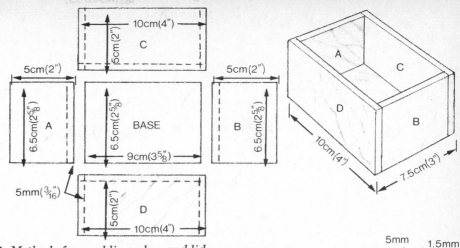

7. *Method of assembling a box and lid.*

□ Hand polish the top of the base and the inner surfaces of the two sides with felt or leather and tin oxide and water (see Lapidary chapter 6), or polish them on a lapping unit (see Lapidary chapter 7). After polishing, remove the cellophane tape and clean the slabs thoroughly.

□ Apply epoxy resin to the unpolished strips on sides A and B and place them in position against the corresponding edges of the base (see fig.7). Place in a clamp (the clamp on your saw can be used for this), in order to hold the slabs in position while the glue is drying.

□ When the glue is dry (after about an hour), remove the assembled slabs from the clamp and check that they are correctly aligned. If there is any irregularity, lap each side with coarse grit until base and sides are in line with each other.

□ Taking sides C and D (see fig.7), place them in position against the assembled slabs. Pencil a line across their ends at a level with the upper face of the base and down their sides where they adjoin the first two sides A and B (along the dotted lines indicated in fig.7).

□ Fasten a strip of the tape across their ends and down their sides to align with the pencil marks, and hand polish the inner faces of these sides as before.

□ Remove the strips of tape and apply epoxy resin to the unpolished areas. Position them against the other sides and base, and place in the clamp or secure with rubber bands until the glue is dry.

□ Check the box for any irregularities in alignment; if there are, lap the ends with coarse grit until they are all flush with each other. Make sure that the top edges of the sides are level, especially if you are going to make a lid.

An onyx box like this can be made with or without a hinged lid.

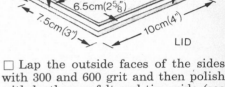

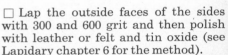

LID

Paul Williams

□ Lap the outside faces of the sides with 300 and 600 grit and then polish with leather or felt and tin oxide (see Lapidary chapter 6 for the method).

□ If you wish to make a lid, take the two thin slabs and lap their faces with coarse grit. Then lap the smaller slab, measuring 9cm x 6.5cm (3⅝" x 2⅝") and 1.5mm (1/16") thick, along each edge so that it fits the opening of the box exactly. Check corners of both slabs with a triangle to insure that all are 90° angles.

□ Lap both faces of each slab with 300 and 600 grit. Polish the edges of the smaller slab and apply epoxy resin to one of its faces and to the same area in the center of the larger slab. Glue the small slab centrally to the under surface of the larger slab, so that there is a 5mm (3/16") distance between the edges of the smaller slab and those of the larger slab (see fig.7).

□ Place a weight on the two slabs until the glue is dry. Then place the lid in the opening of the box to check that the edges of the upper (larger) slab align with the outer edges of the box. Lap any projections with coarse grit until they are flush with the sides of the box.

□ Lap the top, bottom and sides of the box lid with 300 and 600 grit and finally polish with leather or felt and tin oxide.

□ If you wish to hinge the lid, simply glue two hinges of suitable size in position, using epoxy resin. To keep the lid level, glue two small felt pads on the lid opposite the hinges, or glue a flat piece of brass in the middle of the opening edge of the lid. This also enables you to open the box more easily.

Interior design: window treatment

Design know-how 75

Windows are a very important feature in any room, and must be given special attention. During the day, when you rely on natural light for illumination, the windows must be allowed to let in as much light as possible, while at night they must be covered to hide the rather cold, forbidding expanse of glass. The style of window covering you choose must be made to blend in with the rest of the room and there are many alternative methods from which to choose.

Draperies are the most popular form of window covering, perhaps because there are so many different ways of making and hanging draperies, and such a variety of fabrics from which to choose. There are two main ways of hanging draperies—drapery hooks, attached to runners which slot onto a drapery rod or drapery rings sewn onto the top of the drapery, slotted over a long pole above the window. These have been developed into a number of variations of one or the other type and are available in most large department stores. Decorative traverse rods are available in a variety of styles, both traditional and modern. Or you may prefer to use the invisible type of rod, which is covered by the drapery heading. If your windows are fairly tall, you may want to add some horizontal lines in the form of a valance or cornice.

The fabric you choose for your draperies must be suitable for the room, and must be in a color that will blend with your color scheme. When making draperies that will be in direct sunlight during the day, try to find a fabric that will not fade too much. It is possible to buy some very color-fast fabrics that would be good to use for such a window, so be sure to inquire about fading when making your purchase.

When hanging draperies, make sure that the drapery rod comes well beyond the edge of the window so that the draperies can be pulled right back to let in all the available light. This is not possible on certain types of window such as a casement window where another form of window treatment such as window shades may be advisable.

The length of your draperies is another consideration. Floor-length draperies will give a room a rather formal atmosphere, and would look very out of place in certain fabrics and interiors. If you have a room with several small windows on one wall, consider covering all of them with one large drapery. This could have a striking effect when the draperies are drawn, and look much simpler than a lot of small draperies.

Shades and blinds are a form of window treatment which have become particularly popular recently. There are many different types and styles available—window shades, split bamboo blinds, pleated paper shades and venetian blinds in metal, wood or plastic. Choose a style to suit your room—the window shades can be made up in many fabrics but very fine fabrics and those with pile such as velvet are not suitable. Plastic coated fabrics are easy to clean and they make good shades for kitchens and bathrooms. Venetian blinds come in different colors while split bamboo blinds are available in a natural pale brown color.

Kits are available for making window shades and venetian blinds at home which is a cheaper alternative to having them made professionally.

Roman and Austrian shades are more suitable for normal interiors than the other types mentioned. These pull up on tapes—the Roman type into flat pleats and the Austrian type into gathers for a shirred effect. Be careful how you use these shades as they can look very fussy and overdone.

Shutters made of stripped or painted wood can look very attractive in some interiors, giving a clean, uncluttered look. Some have louvers which can be adjusted to let in more or less light and are therefore useful for cutting out bright sunlight as well. During the day they would normally be folded back against the wall.

Shutting out the view. Windows that look out onto an ugly view such as a brick wall (a common fault of urban dwellings) can be permanently covered with such things as venetian blinds, or shutters which will shut out the view but let in the light. Alternatively the glass can be replaced with frosted glass (not very attractive) or the existing glass can be made to look like a stained glass window (see Glass chapter 11, page 1210). Special stained glass kits can be bought which will supply you with fake glass leading and glass paints. The leading is put onto the glass along the lines of a design, and then each section of glass is painted a different color. These fake stained glass windows can look realistic and will cut out an unwanted view successfully.

Liz Whiting

Large bay window fitted with louvered shutters which are used during the day to cut out bright sunlight.

Wind chimes

It is said that wind chimes were originated long ago, by an oriental gentleman. He discovered that by letting certain sea shells hang up in a breeze and so tap together, he drove away all the evil spirits which had plagued his life. Whether this is fact or fallacy, the sound of wind-chimes does have an undisputed charm.

Here is a version, based on the initial idea, made with plastic or metal spoons.

You will need:

Softwood 25mm (1″) thick—one piece 20cm x 20cm (8″ x 8″) and one piece 9cm x 9cm (3½″ x 3½″).
Coping or scroll saw.
Drill with 6mm (¼″) bit.
Metal file.
Fine grade sandpaper.
About 4m (4½yd) colored twine.
14 eyelet screws.
13 plastic or metal spoons.
Scissors.
Compass, protractor, pencil and ruler.
Wood primer and gloss paints or polyurethane varnish.

If you do not have suitable bits of softwood buy scraps. On the larger piece of wood draw a circle with a 9cm (3½″) radius using compass and pencil. Cut out using the coping saw. Smooth rough edges with sandpaper.

Using the protractor make 12 lines at 30° from the center. Make a mark on each line 2cm (¾″) from the outer edge. Using a screw, make a shallow hole at each mark.

Depending on whether you want a varnished wood finish or a painted one, prepare the softwood accordingly.

Into each of the twelve holes on the round piece screw an eyelet screw. Then screw one into the center on each side of the wood.

Take the 13 spoons and file a small notch each side of the handles, close to the

Neil Lorimer

ends. On one spoon file two additional notches about 1cm (½″) from the tip of the scooped part. Paint metal spoons.

Cut the twine into 13 assorted lengths measuring from 20cm (8″) to 30cm (12″). Wind one end of each length around handle notches on spoons, knot end to rest of length, wind twine around again and knot securely.

Using the longest piece of twine for the central spoon (the spoon with four notches) thread end of each length through an eyelet screw, wind around again and fasten with several knots.

Drill a hole near one corner of softwood square. Cut a 30cm (1′) length of twine and wind it around the notches in the scooped end of the central spoon and knot securely. Thread opposite end through hole in softwood square. Knot securely and trim off excess. Hang up the wind chimes with twine.

Decorating with marquetry

The art of marquetry was first practiced in wood, and entailed piecing together flat pieces of delicate wood veneer of different tones and textures to make pictures or to decorate wooden objects by inlaying the veneer in the wood. Paper marquetry is an imaginative and original way of using

This magnificent screen is covered with a marquetry landscape of paper.

Melvin Grey

paper in the same manner, to decorate furniture and other objects.

Using paper for marquetry has the advantage of being easier to handle than wood. It also gives more colorful results and is certainly a great deal cheaper than wood marquetry. If you plan to pursue the craft of wood marquetry, it is a good idea to use paper first in order to get used to the marquetry technique. Paper marquetry can be sealed with varnish to give it a hard, protective surface.

All kinds of wooden objects can be covered with paper marquetry—a picture frame, a cupboard, a screen or a box—but beginners in the craft are advised to start by decorating a small area with a very simple design.

The reverse side of the same screen. Designed by Anita Lear.

The best paper to use is in fact very thin cardboard, which is about 0.5mm ($\frac{1}{40}$″) thick. This, or construction paper of the same thickness which is also suitable, is available in many different colors from art supply stores. It should have a flat or unfinished surface which is suitable for varnishing.

The varnish is applied to protect the design. It also makes it appear as if it were inlaid in the surface onto which the paper is stuck, in the same way as a découpage design is 'sunk' beneath several layers of varnish (see Paper chapters 41 and 42, pages 1654 and 1694 for the method).

The general method. Draw your design on tracing paper rather than directly onto paper of board. The latter methods requires more proficiency and should only be used when the craft has been fully mastered. A soft pencil should then be used to draw the design on paper or board, and erased before the final varnishing stage.

Confine your first attempts at marquetry to covering areas of about 20cm x 30cm (8″ x 12″), or smaller. Try not to work with paper pieces larger than about 30sq cm (12sq in) because it is very difficult to get an even surface if the pieces are larger than this. The paper may buckle when varnished and parts of the design will then not fit together properly, or some parts of the

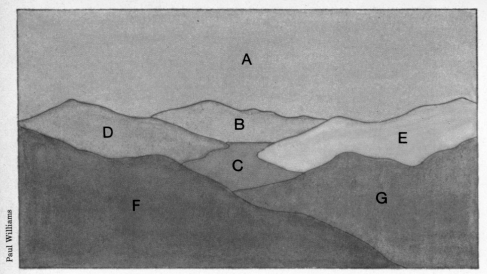

1. *Landscape design for a box, using seven pieces of paper of different colors*

glued paper may set before others, and this will cause difficulties. It is important to work with great accuracy in order to obtain really good results; it is also essential to work in clean surroundings.

A landscape

The following directions are for a small landscape, similar in style to that on the screen (see previous page), but intended to cover the lid of a wooden box. The design uses seven different colors, whereas the landscape on the screen uses eight for each side. Both have the paler colors at the top and the stronger colors in the foreground. This gives the impression of distance required in a landscape.

You do not have to copy the design given here exactly, but bear in mind that in fig.1 area A is intended to be the sky, area C the sea or a lake, and the rest are hills.

Because the process involves cutting two or more pieces of paper or cardboard simultaneously, always work from the top to the bottom of a design because this simplifies the cutting out. Try to plan the design so that you cut through as few thicknesses of paper or cardboard as possible.

You will need:
Seven different colored pieces of cardboard or similar, lettered A to G, according to the colors you want for a particular section of the design.
Water soluble white glue. (This kind of glue is ideal for paper marquetry on wood since it forms a good bond between the two materials and dries fairly rapidly.)
Varnish such as acrylic polymer varnish. (This water-based varnish looks rather like milk and can be bought in either flat or gloss finish from most art stores. Ordinary varnish changes the color of paper and can

mottle the colors, but acrylic polymer varnish does not affect the color.) Lacquer or glaze can be used instead of varnish. They do not change the color of paper or cardboard.
A roll of gummed paper tape.
Transparent tape.
A piece of tracing paper at least the size of the box lid.
A soft 2.5cm (1″) brush for varnishing. Piece of cardboard for a glue spreader. A firm, hard cutting board.
Craft knife, pencil, sandpaper, a piece of thin paper to cover the box lid.
To make the design, first draw the outlines of the design on the tracing paper, lettering each area to correspond with the seven colored pieces you are to use (see fig.1).
☐ Place the tracing paper with the design on it over the pieces A and B which should overlap each other (fig.2). Tape the edges of cardboard and

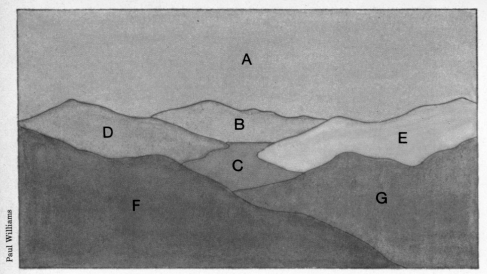

2. *Cut through pieces A and B and tracing paper as indicated.*

paper to the cutting board with the tape.
☐ With the sharp knife, cut as shown by the dotted line in fig.2, through the tracing paper and the pieces A and B. (The point of cutting neighboring pieces together is to ensure greater accuracy in the final fitting together of the section, which

is important in any sort of marquetry.)
Note: the edges of piece A which will adjoin pieces D and E do not have to be accurately cut along the lines on the tracing paper at this stage (see fig.2), because they will be cut later when sections D and E are cut out. Do not trim the outside edge of the picture to size until the final gluing-down stage.
☐ Remove tracing paper and cardboard from the cutting board, and stick the pieces of tracing paper together again on the reverse side as accurately as possible with transparent tape. (You could copy the design onto several sheets of tracing paper in order to avoid sticking it together again, but this is possibly a less accurate method than using the same piece of tracing paper through all stages of cutting.)
☐ Discard unwanted pieces, and carefully stick sections A and B together on the reverse side of the cardboard with pieces of gummed paper tpe (fig.3),

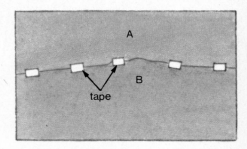

3. *Stick sections A and B together on their reverse side.*

so that their edges meet exactly.
☐ On the board place pieces C with the joined sections A and B over it and the tracing paper on top. Tape all these pieces and the tracing paper to the board.
☐ Following the dotted line in fig.4,

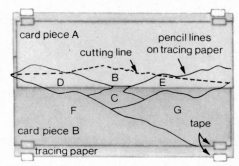

4. *Cut through pieces B and C and tracing paper as indicated.*

cut through the two layers of cardboard and tracing paper, accurately where section B meets section C.
☐ Discard unwanted pieces.
☐ Stick the pieces of tracing paper together again on the reverse side with transparent tape.
☐ On the reverse side of cardboard, stick section C to section B with

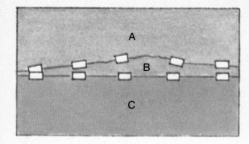

5. *Stick sections B and C together on their reverse side.*

gummed paper tape (fig.5).
☐ Place piece D on the board under joined sections A, B and C, with the tracing paper on top. Tape all these pieces of cardboard and the tracing paper to the board.
☐ Following the dotted line in fig.6

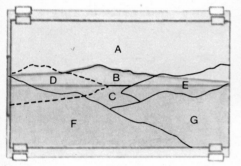

6. *Cut through pieces A, B, C and D and tracing paper as indicated.*

around area D, cut through the layers of paper and cardboard, discard unwanted pieces and stick the pieces of tracing paper together again.
☐ Stick the sections of cardboard together on the reverse side with gummed paper tape (fig.7).

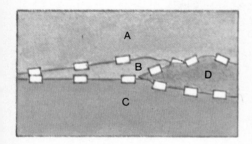

7. *Stick section D to sections A, B and C on reverse side.*

☐ Repeat the process with pieces E, F and G in turn, following the lines on the tracing paper and joining them to the rest of the design with gummed paper tape.
To glue the design to the box lid, first sandpaper the lid smooth.
☐ Working fairly quickly, coat the lid with a thin layer of glue, using a piece

of cardboard. The glue must not be on so thickly that it seeps up between the sections of cardboard, nor so thinly that they will not stick to the box. Place cardboard carefully over the box lid, starting at one corner and working to the other corners. If glue should seep through, wipe it off immediately with a cloth.
☐ Place a piece of thin paper over the marquetry to keep it clean, and rub your fist all over it to maintain an even pressure for about a minute. If the lid is really flat, place a heavy weight on the protective paper and leave it for about five minutes. However, make sure that no glue has seeped through the cracks in the cardboard you are doing this, and that the thin paper does not stick to the design.
☐ Trim the edges of the marquetry to fit the box. When the glue is thoroughly dry the design can be varnished.
To varnish the design, dilute a small amount of the varnish with the same amount of water and apply the first coat quickly and evenly with the soft brush. Do not saturate cardboard or it will split into layers. The milky-colored varnish clears when it dries and the colors of the cardboard can be seen again.
☐ When the varnish is dry, repeat three times with undiluted varnish.

Melvin Grey

Jewelry box lid with detail (above).

Straight-edged patterns
If sections of straight-edge patterns are needed, for a picture frame or for a design similar to that on the jewelry box shown, the method is very simple.
☐ Cut the pieces of cardboard in your chosen colors into long strips and place the strips side by side on wet gummed paper.
☐ When the gummed paper is dry, cut across the strips as desired, either crosswise or diagonally (fig.8). Large or small areas of pattern can be made quickly this way.

8. *For straight-edged patterns, cut across strips of paper and arrange as desired.*

A ceramic doll's head

Doll designed by Islington Dolls.

The first stage in making a ceramic doll's head is to sculpt an original model out of gray clay, see Clay chapters 27, page 1206 and 28, page 1238. The head can, and indeed should, be to your own design but you should aim for rounded, almost blunt features, not sharp definition. The second stage is to make a cast around your clay model and the third stage is to cast the final head in the mold.

Heads can be cast in almost any size—the one in the photograph is about 15cm (6") high, including the breastplate. It has been attached, by means of holes in the breastplate, to a rag body and has been given clothes and a wig to complete its personality.

The doll's head

When buying materials, you will find that both casting plaster and casting slip come in large quantities, enough to make more than a dozen heads of the size of this one.

You will need:
About 6kg (12lb) prepared gray clay.
Modeling tools.
Potter's sponge.
Bowl of water.
Fin casting plaster (a kind of Plaster of paris)—about 10kg (20lb).
Casting slip—which comes in 8½ liter (1 gallon) tubs.
Four pieces of varnished wood, each about 6mm (¼") thick, 45cm (18") long and 30cm (12") high.
Four L plates or brackets.
Screwdriver and 4 screws.
Plastic bucket, jug.
Sharp knife and fettling knife.
Soft-haired paintbrush.
2 very large rubber bands.
2 strips of wood, about 2cm (1") wide and long enough to support cast over bucket.
Awl or sharpened screwdriver to make holes in breastplate.
Wooden board, about 20cm (8") square.
Turntable, optional, to stand head on while modeling.

Sculpting the head

☐ Use wooden modeling tools to sculpt a head and shoulders, about 15cm (6") high in total, out of gray clay. Sculpt rounded features because sharp ones may break off in the cast.

☐ Leave the head until it is dry but not completely hardened.

☐ Using clean water, gently sponge over the entire model to ensure a completely smooth surface (fig.1).

Making the cast

☐ Wedge some clay into a rough square, which must be 2cm (1") wider than the widest part of the model, in this case the shoulders.

☐ Lie the model, face upward, on this bed of clay with the shoulders right at the bottom edge. (The bottom shoulder edge will eventually form the aperture of the mold.)

☐ Gradually build clay up around the model, following the contours, but leaving the base uncovered.

Do not build higher than the ears, but make sure the model is embedded up to the highest part of the dome of its head—that is to say, the point on the dome which is highest when the model stands upright. This is crucial, because if you build too high, or not high enough, at this stage, you will not be able to remove the finished head from the cast.

☐ Use a modeling tool to smooth the clay in around the head (fig.2).

The embedding clay must be absolutely smooth at this point because it will form the edge of the plaster cast. Unevenness could mean that the two halves of the cast will not fit comfortably together.

☐ Use your thumbs to make an indentation near each of the two top corners of the clay bed. These are known as key notches and will enable you to fit the two halves of the cast perfectly together.

The casting box must now be assembled in order to make the first half of the mold.

☐ Make sure that the four walls of the clay block are square so that the casting box will fit neatly around them.

☐ Screw an L bracket into each end of the long side of each piece of wood so

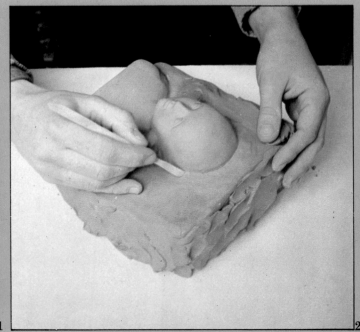

2163

that the adjoining piece of wood can be slotted into it (fig.3).

☐ Assemble the casting box around the clay block by slotting the L brackets over the wooden walls (see fig.3).

☐ Once this retaining wall is in place, secure the corners, the insides and outsides of all joins and the base with clay to prevent the plaster from leaking out.

Mixing the plaster must be done just before you need it. If in doubt about quantity, always make too much rather than too little. Surplus can be thrown

away, but if you run out half-way through, the project can be ruined.

☐ Put 1½ liters (about 3 pints) of water into a bucket.

☐ Add the plaster by sprinkling it by the handful on the surface of the water. Do not stir it at this stage.

☐ Continue to sprinkle plaster until, instead of sinking, it floats on the surface. Almost at once it will begin to crack, like baked mud.

You must now work very fast indeed, or the plaster will set before you are ready to use it, and it will be wasted.

☐ Put your hand and arm into the bucket and stir the plaster, breaking up any lumps.

☐ Gently vibrate the surface of the plaster with your hand to release any air bubbles.

☐ Pour the plaster gently into the casting box (fig.4). Continue to pour until the head is completely covered.

☐ Allow the plaster to set. This takes about twenty minutes.

☐ Take away the casting box, piece by piece.

☐ Turn over the block of clay and

Nelson Hargreaves

Casting the head

☐ Put the two halves of the mold together so that the key notches lock into each other.

☐ The two halves should fit perfectly. If they don't, tidy up the edges with a fettling knife.

☐ Secure the two halves together with two wide, strong rubber bands. Stand the mold with aperture upward.

☐ Pour the casting slip clay into the mold (fig.7) so that it runs down the

sides. Fill the mold to the brim.

☐ As the clay shrinks into the mold, keep topping it up until the clay around the edge of the opening has dried to a thickness of about 3mm (⅛″).

☐ Pour out excess slip.

☐ Place the two pieces of wood across the top of the bucket and stand the mold, aperture downward, on the wood (fig.8). Leave it to drain for about half an hour.

☐ Remove the rubber bands.

☐ To separate the two halves of the mold, tap as before at the top corners with a palette knife and then gently pull the two pieces apart.

☐ Remove the head and let it dry out to the leather-hard stage.

Finishing

☐ Use the sharp knife to cut off the rounded parts of the shoulders (fig.9) so that the head is supported on the breastplate.

5

6

plaster and remove the bed of clay, leaving the original model embedded in the plaster. The bed of clay will come away easily because it is damper than the clay of the model.

☐ Brush the exposed surface of the hardened plaster with diluted slip clay (fig.5). If you don't do this the second half of the mold will stick to the first and it is essential that eventually they can be parted.

☐ Re-assemble the casting box around the half-embedded model, not forgetting to secure the corners and edges

with clay, as before (fig.6).

☐ Mix another 1½ liters (about 3 pints) of plaster.

☐ Pour a layer of plaster into the casting box to the depth of the first half of the mold.

☐ Let the plaster set for about 20 minutes.

☐ Remove the casting box.

☐ Stand the mold upright, shoulders downward.

☐ The line separating the two halves of the mold will be visible. Gently insert the end of a palette knife between

the two halves, at one corner, and tap the knife sharply.

☐ Repeat the tapping at the opposite corner.

☐ Pull the two halves of the mold apart and remove the original clay head.

☐ With a moistened sponge, wipe away any traces of clay from inside the plaster cast.

Before the mold can be used it must be allowed to dry thoroughly. Leave it to dry out overnight in a nice warm room.

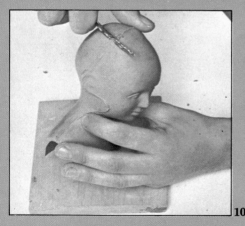

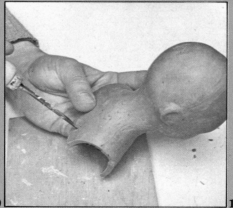

10

11

12

☐ Use the fettling knife to smooth the head seam (fig.10).

☐ Use a drill to pierce four holes in the breastplate, two at the back and two at the front (fig.11). These holes will enable you eventually to attach the head to a cloth body.

☐ Make sure you let the head dry out completely.

☐ For a totally smooth finish, use the sponge wrung out in clean water to wipe, very gently, the fettled seam and

the edges of the breastplate (fig.12). If necessary, you can also sponge the face to ensure that it is completely smooth—but a light touch is absolutely essential or you will blur the features. The head should now be biscuit-fired, glazed and glaze-fired in the usual way. Choose a flesh-colored glaze and, when these stages have been completed, paint in the features with china paints, available from hobby shops. Buy, or make, a wig and glue it in place. The

head is then ready to be attached to a cloth body which can be dressed in any style you choose.

If you wish, you can make clay legs and arms for the doll, using exactly the same techniques as for the head. For the best effect, each clay leg and arm should stop at knee and elbow joints. They should be attached to a cloth upper arm and upper leg by means of holes pierced in the top of each clay piece at the leather-hard stage.

Spinning with a spindle

Materials for spinning need not be elaborate. Fleece, hand carders and a simple drop spindle are all you need.

Although born out of necessity in the past, the skill of spinning is still very much alive. Many weavers especially like to create interesting and unusual yarns for their projects by spinning wool from the raw fleece. However, the yarn produced is just as suitable for knitting or crochet where the strength of the wool is not of prime importance. Evidence shows that the art of spinning emerged early in the history of man, and spun threads are among relics of primitive man. The mummy cloths from Egyptian tombs are woven from finely-spun flaxen threads and recent excavations in Switzerland have revealed finely-spun and woven scraps of wool cloth dating back to 3000 BC.

Materials

Until the 16th century and the invention of the spinning-wheel, the spindle was the only equipment generally available for spinning wool. The simple drop spindle is just a wooden stick with a notch at the top and a disk attached near the bottom. It is the most primitive of spinning equipment and is especially suitable for beginners as it does not demand considerable outlay. The more advanced spinning wheel is described in the next chapter. Spindles can be bought fairly cheaply from specialist suppliers, but if you have a scroll saw and a brace and bit, making a spindle is very easy.

To make a spindle
You will need:
A piece of doweling 30cm (12″) long and 1cm (⅜″) thick.
Piece of wood not less than 10cm (4″) square and about 1.25cm (½″) thick for the disk or whorl.
Scroll saw.
Brace with 1cm (⅜″) bit.
Sharp penknife.
Sandpaper.
☐ Using the scroll saw, make a disk 7.5cm (3″) in diameter. Smooth down the edges with sandpaper.
☐ Drill a hole in the center of the disk using the brace and bit.
☐ Push the dowel rod through this hole until a little less than 2.5cm (1″) shows under the disk.
If you have made a hole that is too large a little plasticine will hold the

dowel rod in place. The hole may need sanding if it is too small.
☐ Using the knife, cut a notch 2cm (¾″) from the top-end of the piece of doweling.
☐ Shape and smooth this end of the dowel rod with the knife and sandpaper.
Raw wool, or fleece, can be bought undyed, ready sorted and in small amounts of about 250gm (8oz) suitable for the handspinner. These small quantities are known as matchings and are graded according to diameter of fiber. You can also buy commercially prepared fleece ready for spinning. This has generally been washed and combed. Suppliers sometimes list this material as rovings.
A small quantity of fleece should be bought to begin with—about 1kg (2½lb) is recommended. Whole fleeces can also be bought but as they weigh on average about 3kg (6lb) it is best to buy the

1. *Tease or pick the fleece by separating the fibers and picking out any dirt.*

small amounts to practice with. Wool gathered from barbed wire is not recommended as weathering destroys the essential natural oils.
Because sheep vary so considerably, the color and texture of fleeces offer a range of choice to the handspinner. Natural colors can range from almost white through cream and brown to black and white.
When woven or knitted undyed, these tones may be used in contrast to produce attractive combinations and subtle variations.

Preparing the wool
The wool must first be picked and carded to separate the fibers and prepared for spinning by forming a roll of wool, a roving or rolag. Wool contains natural oils essential to the texture—and the oils should not be washed out of it before spinning.
To pick or tease wool, take a small amount and gently pull it out until the fibers resemble gossamer. As you do this, pick out any dirt that still clings to the fibers (fig.1).
Carding wool is a process which separates the fibers and makes them all lie in the same direction. You will need two carding combs or cards. Modern cards are square hand-held instruments that have a working surface covered with a thick cloth or leather through which wire bristles

project. The earliest hand cards were really frames on which wild teasles were attached—hence the term carding or teasing the wool. The cards separate the wool fibers by catching them between the wire bristles.

☐ Take one of the cards in your left hand and hold it so that the handle points to the left, away from your body, and the wired area toward you and

2 and 3. *Place fleece on left-hand carder and draw right-hand one across it.*

upright.

☐ With your right hand, spread enough of the teased wool across the teeth of the card you hold to just cover the teeth (fig.2).

☐ Gripping the other card in your right hand, draw the teeth of the right

card quickly and lightly across the teeth of the left card in a stroking movement (fig.3).

☐ Repeat this action five or six times. In this way, the point-to-point action of the bristles reduces the fibrous mass to a fine state evenly distributed on both working surfaces of the cards. The action pulls all the fibers into a uniform direction.

4. *Use the backs of the cards to roll the carded fleece into a rolag.*

☐ Reverse the action once and the wool will come away from the lower teeth. The resulting mass of fibers should be gently rolled between the backs of the cards or between the hands into a cylindrical shape called a rolag (fig.4). Set the rolag to one side and card some more of the wool.

Spinning

Before spinning you will need to prepare by hand about 45cm (18″) of wool thread from a rolag. This is very important as it not only gives the spinner a feel of the process but also the much-needed confidence before using the spindle.

☐ Take a rolag in your left hand and

with your right pull a few fibers. As you pull them, twist counter-clockwise to form a short, thin thread (fig.5).

☐ Secure this small thread on something firm such as a hook and continue to twist in an counter-clockwise direction using both hands so that the thread grows longer.

☐ The thread is highly liable to pull apart and break in places at first. When this happens, overlay the last 2.5cm (1″) with fibers from the rolag and, while holding the weak point between the finger and thumb of the left hand, continue to twist.

5. *Before spinning on a spindle, 45cm (18″) of yarn must be prepared by hand.*

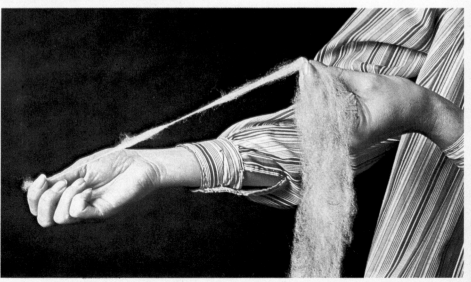

☐ When at last the thread measures 45cm (18″), unhook the end and tie it around the spindle so that it is secured a little above the whorl (fig.6).

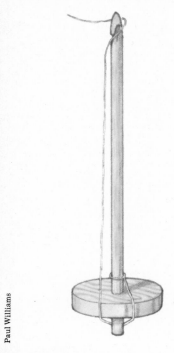

Paul Williams

6. *Threading the spindle.*

☐ Take the yarn down over the edge of the whorl, and around the dowel rod.
☐ Bring the yarn up over the whorl again to the notch at the top of the dowel rod as shown.
☐ Secure the yarn around the notch with a knot.
The spindle is now ready for use.
Spinning sequence. Place the rolag over the back of the right hand, pinching out the thread between the first finger and thumb (fig.7).
☐ With your left hand twist the

spindle sharply clockwise from the base and making sure that the spindle is clear of the ground (fig.8).
☐ The twist from the spindle can be felt as it meets the right hand. At this point, move the left hand up and pinch the thread a little below the right hand (fig.9).
☐ Pull out a few more of the fibers before pinching the thread again and releasing thread with left fingers.
The sequence to follow is:
turn spindle, left hand;
pinch fibres, left hand;
pull out more fibers, right hand;
pinch, right hand;
release left hand for spinning spindle.
☐ An easy rhythm should emerge with practice. Overlay threads from a new rolag as the first one comes to an end.
☐ As more yarn is spun the spindle will reach the floor. Stop spinning and unhitch the yarn from the top and bottom of the spindle.
☐ Wind the yarn around the dowel rod between the whorl and notch, criss-crossing it to form a cone shape so that the spindle is balanced.
☐ Leave 45cm (18″) unwound to start the process all over again but make sure that you do not put so much yarn onto the spindle that it will not spin in a balanced way.
☐ When the spindle is full, wind the

yarn off on to the upright back of a chair leaving 45cm (18″) unwound.
☐ Retie this length to the spindle.
☐ Remove the skein and tie loosely in four places.
Washing the wool. Before the wool can be made up it must be washed.
☐ Prepare a bowl of warm water and add pure soap or soap flakes such as recommended for washing delicate wool garments.
☐ Soak the skeins for twenty minutes, squeeze gently and rinse in warm water.
☐ Repeat this three times and after the final rinse, cut the ties and rewind the wool onto the back of the chair to dry and stretch. (Do not use a polished wooden chair unless it is protected by a plastic bag.)
☐ Do not dry the wool in any heat as it will shrink and become matted.

Using your yarn
Yarn spun on a spindle is ideal for knitting and crochet, especially when the slight variations in natural tones are exploited in subtle shading.
With practice and skill in using the spindle it is possible to produce a yarn suited for weaving both in texture and strength. However, it is hard for the beginner to achieve the uniform tension in the twist that is needed when weaving a fabric in handspun wool.
The unevenness and knotted texture of this yarn, however, makes it an excellent feature in the weft. Individual threads or even lengths of unspun fleece can be inserted in the weft and held in position by a couple of rows of plain weave. Some remarkable effects can be achieved with the imaginative use of handspun yarn in combination with commercial yarn. This is why the process of spinning is so highly attractive to the weaver.

7, 8 and 9. *As the spindle is twisted, pull fibers from the rolag.*

Paul Kemp

Liming, pickling, fuming, scorching

Fashion has always had a strong influence on furniture, on its makers and on the finishing techniques applied to wood. Today, an antique look to wooden furniture in the house is prized as it makes a comforting contrast to the many bald, boring factory finishes on the market.

This chapter discusses ways of reproducing several antique finishes—liming, fuming, pickling and scorching—on new wood. Some of the methods are, however, equally suited to the repair of antique surfaces.

Liming

Traditionally, this process is carried out on oak. The purpose of the process is to emphasize the full beauty of the wood's grain. It involves filling all the surface pores and grain lines with finely ground lime so that they show up in sharp contrast to the wood.

There are two additional benefits to be gained from liming: the filling of the surface of the oak with lime makes it a good deal smoother than if it had been left untreated. Also, the lime and water paste used partially bleaches the natural yellowness out of the wood, leaving it a very attractive gray-brown.

Lime does not react well to being sealed, so if you need to put a protective finish on your limed wood it is advisable to forget about authenticity and use an alternative filler.

Plaster-based wood fillers, which are sold in paste form, give a similar finish to the wood as does lime. Alternatively, you can get a more brilliantly contrasting white finish by mixing titanium white powder—a metallic powder—with a modern, transparent wood filler or a polyurathane (plasticized) grain filler. These are dealt with later on in the chapter.

The drawback with these alternative types of filler is that they do not bleach the wood as does the lime.

Liming is only really effective on woods that have an open surface, such as oak, elm and most mahoganies. Beech and other close-grained fruitwoods may not take the finish so well. To make the surface indentations more pronounced, it is often a help to brush the wood along the grain with a fine

wire brush. This requires care as torn fibers, resulting from uneven, hasty brush strokes, can be difficult to smooth.

You will need:
Hydrated (garden) lime and water. This is available from gardening equipment suppliers or drugstores.
Note: lime is a caustic substance and could damage the skin on your hands, so wear rubber gloves when working with it. Take care not to get any lime in your eyes and protect the work floor if it is wooden or carpeted.
Coarse cloth, fine steel wool and fine grade sandpaper.
Fine wire brush—optional.
Rubber gloves.
White french polish.
White wax polish—this is made from a paraffin wax and mineral spirits to which is added zinc white powder. The zinc increases the white deposit in the wood grain.
Alternative fillers to lime—a plaster-based wood filler in a paste form diluted according to manufacturer's directions; titanium white powder and a polyurethane grain filler.

☐ Prepare the wooden surface to be limed, making sure that it is clean and free from dust. If necessary, accentuate the grain using the wire brush.

☐ Put .9kg (2lb) of hydrated lime in 3.5 liters (6 pints) of water. Mix until it resembles a stiffish paste. This should be sufficient to cover a fairly large table.

☐ Using a coarse cloth or steel wool, rub the paste into the wood. Use a circular motion when rubbing to ensure that all the surface pores and indentations are filled.

☐ When the lime is semi-dry, wipe off any surplus with a cloth, wiping across the grain.

☐ When the lime is thoroughly dry, smooth the surface with the fine grade sandpaper. Remove the residue filler with fine steel wool then wipe with a clean cloth.

Finish. Apply a coat of white french polish followed by a white wax polish. The wax polish should be made from paraffin wax and mineral spirits. If you wish to increase the white deposit effect of the liming, zinc white powder should be added to the wax polish.

Alternative fillers. The traditional lime finish is best suited to decorative furnishings as it cannot be coated with a protective finish. A similar-looking finish which can be sealed can be obtained by using a plaster-based wood filler such as described previously. The powder is mixed with water until it forms a stiffish paste. It is applied exactly as the lime. After the final smoothing and wiping it can be sealed with a commercial sealer.

Titanium white powder filler is useful if you want a brilliantly contrasting white finish. Mix titanium white powder with a commercial transparent polyurethane wood filler. The mixture is then rubbed into the wood in the same way as the lime. When dry, it is sanded and wiped clean for the sealing process.

Protective finish. Both the plaster-based and titanium powder fillers present no problems for modern sealing finishes. Bear in mind that polyurethane finishes, though labeled 'clear', are slightly golden-brown in color and should be avoided.

A suitable alternative to the polyurethane finish is a commercial acid catalyst lacquer that is water-clear. This is a durable two-part product which requires you to mix the lacquer and catalyst together immediately before use. The mixed solution does not remain usable for more than a few hours. Apply according to the manufacturer's instructions.

Fuming

A traditional method of staining wood, fuming entails exposing the wood to the fumes given off by certain chemicals. Used mostly for oak, it turns the wood a deep, gold brown. Difficulties arise in getting a uniform shade which can vary from light to an almost black tone.

The fumes emitted by many chemicals will darken wood but most present some difficulty with their toning capabilities. Another problem involved with chemical finishes is that they may affect finishes applied after the toning process has been carried out. Also, many toners leave behind noxious residues that are difficult to wash out of the wood. The final effect is not entirely predictable with any of them, but fuming with ammonia does offer some degree of control.

Ammonia has long been favored as a chemical toner for hardwoods, mainly because it does not remain in the wood long after it has done its work. Another reason is that it does not raise the grain fibers too markedly, nor does it require any neutralizing process before the wood can be finished.

To fume wood, prepare an air-tight box or chamber, large enough to stand

The settle has been fumed, the cupboard limed and the chair stripped.

the wood in. The wood is stood on end on a grid over a receptacle containing the ammonia. Alternatively, the wood can be suspended over the ammonia.

Either way, the essential thing is to subject the wood to the fumes as they rise from the ammonia.

How quickly the effect is achieved depends on how efficiently the fumes are trapped so that they do their utmost to the wood before escaping. Fuming on a large scale is not easily performed at home. If you have a lot of wood you want fumed, take it to a firm that deals with it.

In most cases the need to fume wood arises when you wish to repair fumed-wood furniture. The piece of wood used in the repair must be fumed before the

1. *Pickling a pine cabinet by painting on dilute nitric acid.*

2. *The acid is neutralized with a solution of soda and water.*

The cabinet with a pickled finish.

Geoffrey Frosh

renovation begins.

Fuming is not a living-room job but one to be carried out in the best-ventilated outbuilding you can find, or preferably out of doors. This goes for most work involving fumes or sprays, since even those not in themselves noxious can suffocate you if worked with in a badly ventilated space.

You will need:

A concentrated solution of ammonia.

A receptacle for the ammonia—two or three saucers or a soup dish will do.

Old coat-hangers, garden stakes or other pieces of wood. These are for suspending the wood to be fumed or for making the grid.

A large air-tight chamber—a packing case or a tent of large plastic dropcloths.

☐ Pour ammonia into the receptacle. Be careful not to inhale the fumes or spill it on yourself as it can irritate your skin.

☐ Place the piece of wood to be fumed over the container of ammonia. It can either be hung from the coat-hangers or placed on a grid made from the garden canes or other scraps of wood.

☐ Place the tent or packing case over the container and piece of wood. The aim is to concentrate the fumes around the wood.

☐ Keep checking the wood until it is toned to the extent you desire then remove from the fumes.

Alternative: you do not have to use the traditional fuming technique, but can simply apply the ammonia to the wood with a cloth. However, be prepared for a much darker shade than would be achieved with the traditional method.

Note: wear protective rubber gloves while doing this and work in a well-ventilated room.

Pickled finish

This term can be applied to more than one finishing technique. Perhaps its oldest application is to the plaster of paris 'finish' that was left behind when old, lacquered finishes had been stripped off softwood furniture with vinegar. The surface of the pine (as the wood almost invariably was) originally had to be treated with plaster of paris to make it smooth enough for painting. The 'pickle' used by later generations to remove the deteriorating lacquer did not affect the firmly adhering plaster (known as 'spackle'). Consequently, the spackle remained in the broad, spring growth rings of the wood, accentuating the grain pattern. A less pronounced but similar effect was often produced on pine that had been bleached with lime solutions. White, powdery residues in the soft grain channels were difficult to remove and tended to remain on view. Today, the pickled finish found on pine

is caused by dilute nitric acid (see box) which is painted onto the wood. This deepens the color of the pine, improving the contrast between the narrow, hard bands of summer growth and broad, soft bands of the spring growth. The technique can be used on other softwoods.

You will need:

A dilute solution of nitric acid—two parts acid to eight parts water.

A glass or porcelain container for the acid.

An old paintbrush.

Washing or sal soda.

Grade 1/0 sandpaper.

☐ Clean the wood and, working along the grain, put the acid solution on as evenly as possible with a brush (fig.1).

☐ Once you have the shade you want, neutralize the acid with a strong solution of washing soda and water—two parts soda to one part water—(fig.2). Rinse with clean water.

All these steps serve to raise the grain, but that is part of the desired effect of pickled wood. The surface can be lightly smoothed with 1/0 grade sandpaper.

Scorching

Another way to accentuate both color and grain in pine and similar softwoods is to scorch the surface of the wood lightly with a blowtorch (fig.3). For an even charring all over, attach a fish-tail nozzle to the blowtorch. The soft spring growth chars more readily than

the hard, and subsequent wire brushing gives a seamed effect by digging out the spring growth rings (fig.4).

The surface can then be clear-sealed with a polyurethane varnish or waxed (see Finishes chapter 1, page 72). Further variations can be achieved by putting on a thin coat of paint and wiping off the excess with a rag before it dries.

A gray paint used like this will give a driftwood effect, and pale yellow or tan paint a lighter, blond shade. Bronze powder color mixed with clear lacquer adds a special beauty of its own to the wood.

These painted techniques can be used without scorching first if you want a smoother finish.

Although the strength of acid solution required for pickling is only 20% nitric acid, it is still a dangerous chemical to handle. Ideally you should buy it ready diluted to the required strength, but, if you have to dilute the solution yourself, always add the acid to the water, a little at a time so that the heat generated can disperse more safely. Wash off any splashed acid with a lot of water.

Never add the water to the acid: the heat generated when the two mix is enough to 'boil' the water making it splutter and splash you.

3. *Scorching with a blowtorch.*

4. *Charred rings are brushed out.*

Paul Kemp

The art of 'cloisonné'

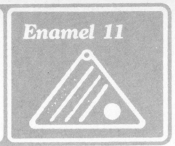
The term 'cloisonné' comes from the French word *cloison*, meaning partitioned area. The term is used in enameling to refer to partitions or fences of rectangular flat wires, placed along the lines of the design and then fixed by various methods to the metal base. The cells formed between these wires are filled with enamels of the desired colors, each *cloison* being quite separate from its neighbor.

Greek goldsmiths produced the first *cloisonné* enamels in the 4th and 5th centuries BC, but the most beautiful *cloisonné* works were Byzantine gold enamels of the 9th to 11th centuries. One of the most outstanding examples of Byzantine workmanship is the Pala d'Oro now in St Mark's Cathedral, Venice.

Cloisonné is a technique still practiced today by many enamelers: it is especially suited to making jewelry.

Metal for 'cloisonné'

Fine (ie pure) silver is an excellent metal for *cloisonné* as it has no added metals to cause oxidation and discoloration of the enamels when firing. Sterling silver (an alloy of 925 parts silver and 75 parts copper) and copper go black with oxidation. This necessitates cleaning off the metal after each firing. Beautiful results, however, are possible with thorough cleaning.

Fine silver or copper rectangular *cloisonné* wires, in various sizes, can be bought ready made.

Traditional 'cloisonné'

In traditional *cloisonné* work the wires are annealed (Enamel chapter 10, page 2148) to make them pliable and then shaped along the lines of the design by manipulating them with the fingers, pliers or tweezers. Wires are then soldered to the base and the ends of the wires soldered together (soldering silver is covered in a later chapter). The silver peacock feather pendant (page 2176) was made in this way.

The enamels are washed and laid wet into the *cloisons*.

As enamel shrinks on firing, the *cloisons* are refilled and re-fired until the level of the enamel reaches the level of the *cloisonné* wires, or just above. The whole surface is then rubbed with a flat carborundum stone under running water until it is quite level. Refiring then gives a glossy surface.

Concave cloisonné. The peacock feather pendant was finished by leaving the cells semi-filled. This method, known as concave *cloisonné*, gives added reflections which looks most attractive on jewelry.

This exotic 'cloisonné' dish and stand was made in China at the beginning of the twentieth century.

Silver wire on copper

A method of making *cloisonné* which does not involve soldering is used for making the pear-shaped pendant. Shaped silver wires are embedded into the first coat of enamel—silver grade transparent flux—thus avoiding soldering them in position.

The pendant is made from a pre-formed copper blank with silver wires forming the *cloisonné* work.

You will need:

Equipment. See Enamel chapter 1, page 106, plus an enameling stilt.

Materials. Pear-shaped copper blank 7.5cm (3″) overall length with a hole for a jump ring.

Fine silver rectangular *cloisonné* wire 1.5mm x .31mm (.06″x .012″). (If rectangular wire is not available use a round fine silver wire.)

Counter enameling powder.

Gum tragacanth (see Enamel chapter 5, page 514) or other enamel adhesives.

Round and square copper studs—various sizes.

Paintbrush.

Silver enamel flux.

Transparent enamel in chosen colors.

Copper chain and jump ring.

Flat Carborundum® stone pencil.

Salt and vinegar pickle solution.

Very fine wet-or-dry paper.

Tripoli and rouge (optional).

Silver cleaning brush (soft nailbrush).

Fine file.

Wire cutters.

Tweezers.

Jewelry pliers (optional).

Polishing grade abrasive paper, grades No. 240, 400, 600.

Non-abrasive commercial silver polish which will not damage the enamel (optional).

☐ Switch on the kiln so that it is hot enough to use, ie bright orange, by the time you are ready to fire.

☐ Clean copper blank in salt and vinegar pickle (1 teaspoonful of table salt to half a cup of vinegar) for a few minutes and/or then rub both sides with emery paper. Swill under the tap and then dry with a clean cloth. Do not get finger grease on the surface.

☐ Paint back of blank with gum and sift on counter enameling powder.

☐ Pick up pendant carefully without disturbing the counter enameling powder: slip a palette knife under the piece and pick up by the edges with your fingers. Turn over the piece very carefully and place it on the stilt.

☐ Dust silver flux on to the upper surface. With a brush, clear any enamel powder which may have fallen onto the stilt.

☐ Place stilt on wire mesh (a planche) on top of kiln to dry out the gum.

☐ When dry, fire piece (on stilt and mesh), until enamel is glossy.

It is worth persevering with this method of firing counter enamel and surface base coat together as it saves work, time and electricity.

☐ When cool, clean the fire-scale from the edges of the piece with a fine file or Carborundum® stone.

☐ Draw around the pendant on paper and create your design. Alternatively trace the design from the photograph. The lines of the design should be curved and flowing and never cross. Avoid sharp angles and narrow straight cells —they tend to crack the enamel.

☐ Switch off, or unplug, the kiln and allow to cool until the chamber has a dull red glow. If kiln is too hot silver wire will melt when placed in it.

☐ Switch on kiln again and anneal the *cloisonné* wire to remove 'springiness' and make it pliable.

Place wire on stilt and planche before putting it in kiln. Do not overheat wire or it could melt, ie remove when it is the same dull red as the firing chamber.

☐ Shape the wire over your drawing using fingers, tweezers or fine jewelry pliers. The pieces of wire can be of any length but must have at least one curve before they will 'stand up': a straight piece of rectangular wire would fall flat. Cut wire with wire cutters.

☐ Transfer the shaped wires to the pendant and glue them carefully in place with the gum.

☐ Place pendant on stilt and planche and then dry out gum by placing it on top of kiln.

☐ Cool the kiln to dull red glow and then, when adhesive is dry, fire the piece until the wires just begin to sink into the coat of flux. Take great care not to overfire or the *cloisonné* wires will melt and appear to sink right down into the enamel, eventually firing out altogether, leaving a horrible mess. Keep the kiln at this low temperature, by switching off from time to time, for the rest of the firings.

☐ Clean the edges with the file when the piece is cool, and between subsequent firings.

☐ Wash enamels carefully, especially the transparent ones. A good method is to place some dry enamel powder in a deep spoon and run tap water very slowly onto the powder, stirring gently. The water will immediately become cloudy. Allow all the cloudy water to run away, leaving larger clean fragments of enamel behind. Keep washing until no more cloudiness appears. Examine the residue for any opaque white bits and remove them.

☐ Lay in the colors wet, packing in as much enamel as possible. Use a small spatula or palette knife to pick up enamel and position it in the appropriate cell with the end of a paintbrush. If the enamel is too wet it will run where you don't want it to— if it is too dry, the enamel already in the cell will not 'accept' the enamel on the spatula. You will soon learn how wet the mixture should be.

Silver wire 'cloisonné' on a copper blank. The wires are embedded in transparent flux enamel before enameling the pendant. Designer: 'Sienna'.

2175

☐ Place piece on stilt and planche and dry out thoroughly on top of the kiln.

☐ Fire carefully until the enamel has a shiny surface, withdrawing the piece from the kiln at the first possible moment.

☐ When cool, clean edges of copper and then repack the cells with more enamel as the first layer enamel will have shrunk considerably. Dry and re-fire.

☐ Repeat this process until the *cloisons* are full.

☐ Place copper studs and opaque shot colors where required, sticking them in place with a little gum. Dry and then fire until they have just fused into the enamel surface.

☐ When cool, clean the edges of the copper with a fine file. Then polish with successively fine polishing grades of abrasive paper if necessary.

☐ Descale and polish the copper studs using wet fine wet-or-dry paper, which has been filed to a fine point. Clean the

Modern silver peacock feather pendant made using traditional methods. This is an example of concave 'cloisonné'. Designed by 'Sienna'.

This 'cloisonné' and gilt box, in the form of a mythological beast, is about 15cm (6") high and was made in China in the eighteenth century.

silver *cloisonné* wires in the same way. Clean each stud and wire separately taking great care not to scratch the enamel.

☐ Wash the piece with liquid deter-

gent and water to remove all traces of abrasive grit, using a soft silver cleaning brush. Once again take care that enamel is not scratched. Dry on a soft cloth.

☐ Polish with silver polish, then wash and dry as before.

Alternatively, polish with tripoli and rouge.

☐ Attach the chain with a jump ring.

General hints

Polishing with tripoli and rouge.
These two very fine abrasive materials are used to give a professional finish to silver or copper. They can be used for either hand polishing, as described here, or on an electric jewelry polishing machine. (An electric polisher will obviously speed up the process, but excellent results are possible with hand polishing.)

Wrap a piece of chamois around your finger or a stick and rub the chamois on a block of tripoli. Polish the piece of work by rubbing the chamois with tripoli on it over the piece. Then wash off the tripoli with liquid detergent and water, using a silver cleaning brush. Dry with a soft cloth.

Repeat the process with a block of rouge.

Note: always use tripoli first and then the finer abrasive, rouge—not the other way around.

The blocks of abrasive tend to dry out in time. If they do put a little pure oil—any sort will do—on the block of tripoli before rubbing chamois on it. Rouge can be moistened with kerosene in a similar way to tripoli.

How to make a Victorian doll

This chapter gives patterns and directions for making the body of a Victorian doll. The completed body can be attached to several kinds of heads which you can either make and paint yourself or which can be purchased, painted or unpainted.

Whatever kind of head is used, it must have not only a neck, but some kind of breastplate or shoulder piece. Otherwise the head will not sit well on the body and will not be stable.

A cast resin, clay or papier mâché head usually has a breastplate with holes drilled in it. The plate is placed over the top of the body and is stitched in place with large firm stitches, using a double thread.

A head made of wood is usually solid, in which case it is inserted into the top edge of the body and firmly glued to the fabric.

If you are painting the head yourself, it is easier and less risky to paint it before attaching it to the body. Some heads have cast hair, which should also be painted at this stage.

If you are adding a hair or wool wig, do not glue it on until the head has been attached to the body and the doll is dressed and entirely finished, since constant fitting of clothes will spoil the hair-style.

It is advisable to decide on the kind of head you are going to use before making up the body, and to make or

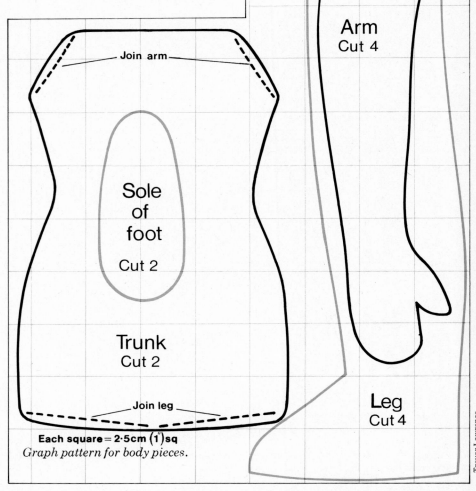

Join arm

Sole of foot
Cut 2

Trunk
Cut 2

Join leg

Each square = 2·5cm (1")sq
Graph pattern for body pieces.

Join body

Arm
Cut 4

Leg
Cut 4

Trevor Lawrence

Peter Heinz

Hand painted papier mâché head.

Solid wooden head with real hair.

Unpainted cast resin head.

purchase it accordingly.

The length of the body shown here is 4¼ times the height of the head and neck. The body pattern given here is for a body about 48cm (19″) tall, which suits a head and neck about 10.5cm (4¼″) high. Use these measurements as a rough guide to check that the body pattern is in correct proportion to the head you have selected. You may find that you have to reduce or enlarge the body pattern accordingly.

Patterns and directions for the doll's clothes are given in the next Cloth chapter. They are not sewn directly onto the body, but are made so that the doll can be dressed and undressed, thus enhancing its value as a toy.

The finished article will not only be an original and exciting toy for your children, but also an object of beauty in itself.

The body
Suitable fabrics

It is advisable to use a soft fabric to make the body, for a flexible life-like effect. Cotton stockinet, which is usually sold in a width of 132cm (52″), is ideal, but you could use a piece of worn sheet. Cloth which is stiff or contains size produces thin stiff limbs, because it does not give when stuffed.

You will need:

Graph paper and pencil for patterns.

0.5m (½yd) of cotton stockinet or a piece of worn sheet 40cm x 80cm (10″ x 32″).

Tea bag.

Matching thread.

Synthetic stuffing or shredded pantyhose for stuffing.

Knitting needle.

☐ Dip the fabric in a tea bath, using one tea bag to 1 liter (1 quart) of boiling water to obtain a delicate flesh tint.

☐ Make paper patterns from the graph.

☐ Cut out all the body pieces in the dyed fabric, allowing an extra 6mm (¼″) all around for seams.

☐ With right sides facing, machine stitch around the edges of the legs, leaving the top and feet edges open.

☐ Insert the soles in the feet, with right sides facing and narrow end to heel, and machine stitch in place. Turn right side out.

☐ With right sides facing, machine stitch around the edges of the arms and trunk, leaving the top edges open. Turn right side out.

☐ Stuff all five pieces from the open top ends. Stuff them firmly, putting in small amounts at a time. Push the stuffing down with the blunt end of a

This beautiful Victorian doll, designed by Audrey Barker, owes much of its success to careful choice of matching fabrics and attention to detail.

Dick Miller

This papier mâché head has a breast-plate with holes drilled in it, and is attached to the body with strong stitches, using a double thread.

knitting needle.

☐ Tuck in the raw top edges of the limbs and overcast them together.

☐ If you are using a head with a breastplate, close the neck edge of the trunk as for the limbs. If you are using a solid head which is to be glued to the inside of the body, simply finish the neck edge by turning in 6mm (¼″) all around and sewing down neatly, and leave open.

☐ Make a large straight stitch at the front and back of the knees and elbows, using a double thread and taking it right through both layers of fabric and the stuffing. This gives the limbs flexibility.

Paul Kemp

□ Work running stitches on the front of the hands to indicate fingers.

□ To attach the limbs to the body, join the hand sewn edges at the tops of the limbs to the relevant parts of the body as indicated by the dotted lines on the graph patterns and sew in place.

□ The body is now ready to be attached to the head and dressed.

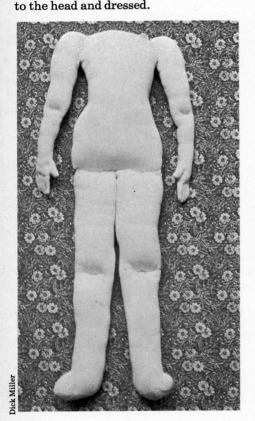

Dick Miller

Finished doll's body, ready for attaching to painted head. The doll should be dressed before attaching the wig.

Painting the head

Cast resin, papier mâché and wooden heads are all painted in the same way. Paint the entire head with white emulsion paint as a base on which to work.

Paint skin, features and hair—if doll has cast hair—using acrylic paint which is fast drying. Mix colored and white acrylic paints to obtain pale delicate shades and dilute with a little water or acrylic medium. It is also possible to use watercolors mixed with white emulsion to obtain the desired colors.

When the paint is dry, you can give the head a coat of non-shiny varnish to make the paint permanent, but this is an optional refinement. Let varnish to dry.

Polish the head with a clean furniture polish for a translucent effect.

Making a wig

Although dolls' wigs can be purchased, they are usually expensive. You can make the doll's 'hair' yourself from an old wig.

Most wigs are made up by machining hair together into a long, very narrow strip or strips stitched onto a net foundation. Remove a strip of hair from the net foundation of the wig (see fig.1).

Measure around the doll's hairline and cut a strip of wig 6mm (¼″) shorter than this length. Glue it to the head, starting 3mm (⅛″) away from the center top of the hairline, wrapping it around to the base of the head and bringing it back up to the other temple, 3mm (⅛″) from the center top of the hairline, thus leaving a 6mm (¼″) gap at the center of the crown.

Repeat this process using shorter and shorter strips of the wig and progressing toward the back of the head until you have covered the sides and back of the head (fig.2). Fill the gap along the center of the head with four straight strips of hair cut to the desired length. This will give the effect of a center part. The hair can then be trimmed and set. Make up a setting lotion by dissolving half a teaspoon of gum acacia crystals—available from most drugstores—in a cupful of warm water. Simply apply this solution to the hair with a cotton swab and set the hair with hair clips. When the hair is dry, remove the clips and brush hair into the desired style. Curls can be catch-stitched in place for permanence.

Hair can also be made from wool. Make a skein of wool 5cm (2″) thick and 35cm (14″) long, and work a row of back stitches across its center to indicate a part. Glue this to the head, matching the part to the center of the head and pull wool down on each side. Put a dab of glue where the doll's ears should be and glue the wool in a bunch to each ear. This will leave a bald patch at the back (fig.3).

Twist the wool up toward the back of the head into a bun to cover the bald patch and catch stitch in place (see fig.3).

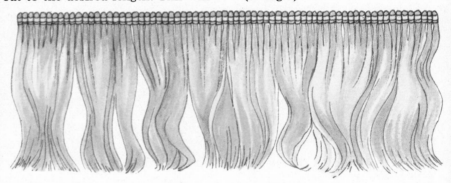

1. *A strip of hair, from the net foundation of an old wig.*

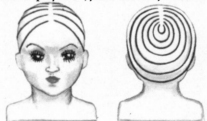

2. *Positioning of strips of hair.*

3. *Bun covers bald patch at back.*

Strips of hair fill central gap.

Geoffrey Frosh

Making patterns with Cavandoli

Cavandoli is a fascinating method of introducing a contrasting color into a piece of macramé otherwise worked in one color. The technique is named after Valentina Cavandoli, an Italian who taught it to young school children in Turin at the end of the 19th century. Cavandoli macramé is worked with one knot throughout—double cording which can be tied in vertical or horizontal knots.

It is a characteristic of all Cavandoli designs that the first and last knots of each row are worked vertically in the contrasting color with a picot (a loop) to link the rows.

Horizontal knots. To tie these, the vertical strands are wrapped around the horizontal strand (fig.1). In Cavandoli

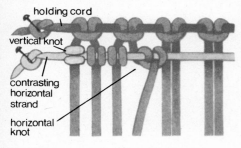

1. *Tying a horizontal cording knot.*

designs this produces the background color.

Vertical knots. These are tied by wrapping the horizontal strand around the vertical strands (fig.2). In Cavan-

2. *Tying a vertical cording knot.*

doli this produces the contrasting color or motif.

Colors. Cavandoli is always worked in two colors—one for the main or background color and one for the

contrasting color or motif. Experiments with two or more contrasting colors are rarely successful unless worked in horizontal bands.

The yarn. Choose a strong firm yarn in a suitable weight for the object you are making—fine yarns for trimmings and watchstraps, string for table mats and bags and chunky ropes and rug wools for floor coverings.

Cavandoli makes a smooth tight fabric so allow eight times the desired length of the article for the background threads with about half the same amount for the contrast thread which is used straight from the ball. For the number of background threads count the number of squares across your design as explained below and halve it.

Designing

Cavandoli can be worked in designs of stripes or checks or you could produce initials or a simple motif. Many of the designs intended for cross stitch embroidery can be translated successfully into Cavandoli macramé.

The best way to plan Cavandoli designs is on graph paper so that one square represents one double cording knot. Mark the design with a cross in each appropriate square of color in the square with crayon. Leave the background squares blank.

Calculating size. To check the number of squares to draw on your chart for a specific size, you should work a small sampler as a practice piece in the yarn you will be using. From this you will be able to measure the number of knots in each direction to 1cm (1″).

Practice piece. To give you some practice at working from a chart as well as making a guide to the knot size, draw a small chart with 20 rows of squares horizontally and vertically. Mark your pattern, with the first and last vertical rows in the pattern color.

☐ From the background yarn cut 10 strands each 1m (40″) long. Attach them to a holding cord in the usual way (Macramé chapter 1, page 176).

☐ Pin the end of the pattern yarn to the left-hand side of the first vertical strand, just below the holding cord. Work a vertical cording knot with the pattern yarn on the first vertical strand (see fig.2).

☐ If the second square on your chart is also a pattern color, work another vertical cording knot with the pattern yarn on the second vertical strand (fig.3a).

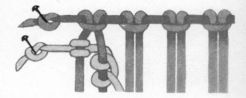

3a. *The second knot tied vertically.*

If, however, the square is blank (indicating background) work a horizontal cording knot with the second vertical strand over the pattern yarn as shown in fig.3b.

3b. *The second knot tied horizontally.*

☐ Continue in this way following your chart, working horizontal or vertical knots as desired. Work the last knot in the row with a vertical double cording knot in the pattern yarn.

☐ The second and following alternate rows are worked from right to left, beginning with a vertical double cording knot. To form the characteristic picot as the link between rows, place a pin to hold the loop (fig.4) and then

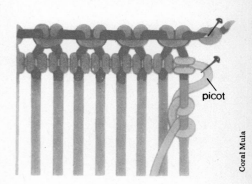

4. *Forming a picot to link the rows.*

work the knot.

☐ Start the third row with the linking picot as before. Continue for the remaining rows of the chart working the appropriate knots.

☐ To finish, either darn back the ends neatly on the wrong side, or cut them to form a fringe, or tie with a firm overhand knot, trim the excess and dab the knot with adhesive to prevent it from coming undone.

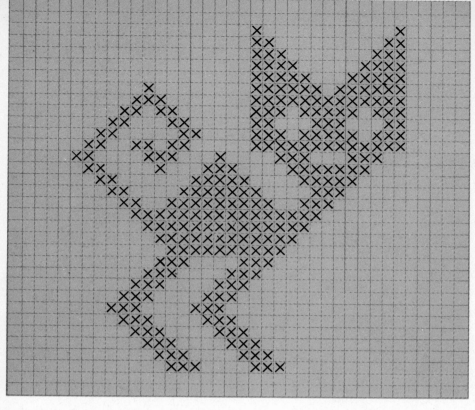

Left: Cavandoli macramé worked in rug wool makes a strong stool cover.

Above: chart for cat motif. Each cross represents one vertical cording knot.

Cat motif

The angular lines of Peruvian cross stitch embroidery, which inspired the cat motif shown opposite, are easy to adapt for Cavandoli macramé. The stool top was worked in rug wool but the motif could also be made up in thinner yarn for a pillow cover.

Man's watchstrap

Size: 2cm ($\frac{3}{4}$″) wide, length to fit an average-sized wrist.

You will need:

14.50m (16yd) crochet thread in main color.

7.50m (8yd) crochet thread in contrasting color.

Buckle, 2cm ($\frac{3}{4}$″) wide.

Macramé board, Push pins.

☐ Cut six 122cm (48″) lengths of thread from main color. Double each length and set onto one of the watch's strap bars. Secure the watch to the macramé board with Push pins crossed over the other strap bar (fig.5).

☐ Roll up the length of contrasting thread and set onto the left of the set-on threads. Work in pattern for 7.5cm (3″). To taper the end, continue working in the pattern but omit one knot at each edge on successive rows until two threads remain. Sew in all the loose threads on the back of the strap.

☐ Cut and set on the same number of threads to the second strap bar and work as before for 7.5cm (3″). Loop the loose threads over the buckle bar and sew them in at the back of the strap. Trim all loose ends.

Woman's watchstrap

Size: 1.2cm ($\frac{1}{2}$″) wide, length to fit an average-sized wrist.

You will need:

7.50m (8yd) crochet thread in main color.

4m (4$\frac{1}{2}$yd) crochet thread in contrasting color.

Buckle, 1.2cm ($\frac{1}{2}$″) wide.

Macramé board, Push pins.

☐ Cut four 90cm (36″) lengths of thread from main color. Double each length and set onto one of the watch's strap bars. Secure the watch to the macramé board with Push pins crossed over the other strap bar (see fig.5).

☐ Roll up the length of contrasting thread and set onto the left of the set-on threads. Work in pattern for 6.5cm (2$\frac{1}{2}$″). Taper the end as described for the man's watchstrap.

☐ Cut and set on the same number of threads for the second strap bar and work as before for 6.5cm (2$\frac{1}{2}$″). Loop the loose threads over the buckle bar and sew them in at the back of the strap. Trim off all loose ends.

Cavandoli in stripes and squares for watchstraps. Designs by Kit Pyman.

Alan Duns

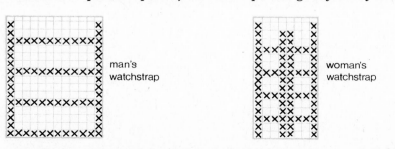

man's watchstrap

woman's watchstrap

Charts for watchstraps. Add or subtract knots to make desired width.

Coral Mula

5. *Pinning the watch to the board.*

Protractors and triangles

line CD (fig.4).
If you want to draw a line longer than the edge of the triangle, butt the edge of a ruler against the edge of the triangle, remove the triangle and draw the line against the ruler.

A triangle and protractor. Notice that the degrees on the protractor are marked in both directions so that angles can be drawn to the left or right.

Angles are measured in degrees. There are 360 degrees in a full circle—an angle of 180 degrees makés a straight line, an angle of 90 degrees makes a right angle. Any angle of less than 90 degrees is called an acute angle. An angle of more than 90 degrees but less than 180 degrees is called an obtuse angle, and an angle of more than 180 degrees is called a reflex angle. A protractor is used to draw and measure angles of any size. For drawing right angles, use a square or triangle.

Protractor
A protractor is a semi-circular plastic disk marked with 180 degrees around the curved edge.

☐ To draw a line from point A (fig.1) at an angle of 35° to line AB, first place the protractor over point A so that the line along the base of the protractor lines up with line AB, and point A is exactly in the center of this line, ie where the line marking the angle of 90° starts.

☐ Find the point marking 35° along the edge of the protractor and, using a sharp pencil, mark this point (X) on the paper (see fig.1).

☐ Remove the protractor. Draw a line from A through point X (fig.2). Line AX will be at an angle of 35° to line AB. This method will work for any angle you may want to draw.

Always use very sharp pencils when drawing angles as this will make your drawings more accurate. Any inaccuracy will become exaggerated as the lines are extended, and your design will become inaccurate as a result.

For drawing right angles the protractor can be used, but a quicker and easier method is to use a square.

A triangle
A triangle is a triangular-shaped piece of wood, or more usually plastic, which has a right angle at one corner. The other angles vary—sometimes they are both 45° and on some triangles they are 30° and 60°.

☐ To draw a line from point C at right angles to line CD (fig.3), first line up an edge of the triangle with line CD, with the right-angled corner of the set square on point C (see fig.3).

☐ Draw along the edge of the triangle. This line is at right angles to

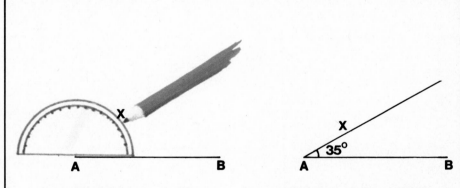

1. *Find 35° and mark point X.*

2. *Draw line from A through point X.*

3. *Place triangle along line CD.*

4. *Draw a line to make right angle.*

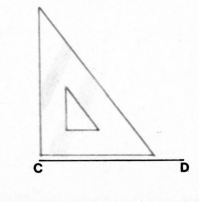

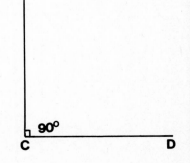

Creative ideas 78

A colorful patchwork wall created in the nursery.

Patchwork wall

Creating a patchwork wall is entertaining and great fun as you can invite friends, your children and their friends to add their painted or crayoned squares. It is a novel way to cover a large, white wall. First decide how large an area you wish to fill and how large the individual squares should be. Then, with a tape-measure and pencil, mark the points on the wall to indicate the corners of the squares. Draw in the sides of the squares against a hard edge, such as a book or ruler.

Choose a square and start decorating. If preferred, simple outlines can be drawn in pencil first. Then combine large, bold brush strokes with fine detail to paint your ideas—you can include doodles, messages and faces.

The best medium to work with is non-drip emulsion paint and this is a good opportunity to use left-over paints. However, wax crayons can be used as an alternative.

For a palette you could use an old plate or cake pan.

Light pencil lines form the squares.

Introduction to papier mâché

Paper 58

Papier mâché is a modeling material consisting of pieces of paper used with paste of glue and molded around a shape to make functional and decorative objects. It is a cheap and easy material to use and has the advantage of drying naturally to a hard and durable substance, without having to be baked like clay.

The craft of making objects from papier mâché is an ancient one. Soon after the Chinese discovered how to make paper, about 2000 years ago, they began to experiment with ways of molding it by tearing it into pieces, mixing it with glue, and shaping it into useful and attractive objects. The interest in this craft declined for hundreds of years until the French revived it in the 18th century. They called it papier mâché, meaning literally 'chewed-up paper'. They used it to make trays, boxes and even furniture (particularly chairs) which were often inlaid with mother of pearl.

All these colorful objects are made of papier maché, using molds ranging from clay to bottles and bowls.

100 Idées de Marie Claire/Capurro

Uses for papier mâché were far more limited then than they are today, since the invention of epoxy resin which makes the papier mâché object much stronger and more durable than traditional water-soluble glues and pastes. Epoxy resin can also be used as a surface finish.

Materials

Most of the materials needed to make papier mâché objects can be found at home.

Paper. The main item is of course paper; old newspapers will probably be your chief source. You can also use paper towels, soft tissues or white

tissue paper. It is worth experimenting, too, with other types of paper such as rag paper, which is stronger than ordinary paper because its ingredients include cotton or linen rags as well as wood pulp. Sources of rag paper include used fine stationery, pages from old ledgers and old damaged books, and drawing papers.

You can also use paper to decorate an object built up from several layers of papier mâché, if you wish. Gift wrapping paper, wallpaper, colored tissue paper and colored magazine pictures are all suitable. In fact, almost any kind of paper may be used.

Pastes and glues. You will also need some kind of paste or glue for binding the paper together to make papier mâché. The one traditionally used for the purpose is a paste made from flour and water which is stirred over a low heat until enough water has been added to make it smooth and creamy. Commercial wallpaper paste, mixed with water according to the manufacturer's directions, also makes a strong glue.

However, epoxy resin, a strong and

The duck and hens were all molded on plasticine and painted in bright colors. Designed by Ruth Beard.

clear glue, is the strongest type to use. It will make papier mâché objects virtually unbreakable, waterproof, fireproof and dirt-proof. It should always be used for large or complex objects without a base support, since they might otherwise buckle.

Using epoxy resin simply as a surface finish for a smaller piece means that the object will not only be protected as if a varnish were used, but it will also be **strengthened** as the glue penetrates the papier mâché itself.

Molds. Some sort of mold will also be required to support the papier mâché object while it is being made. It can either be removed after the papier mâché has dried, or integrated into the piece for added strength. The mold can be either a rigid shape (a plastic bottle, tin can, cardboard cylinder, a glass or china dish or bowl, fruit or vegetables, or even a balloon) or it can be flexible (chicken wire, crumpled newspaper, clay or plasticine).

2187

Methods

There are three basic ways of making papier mâché. The most common is to cut or tear the paper into small strips or squares and glue them onto a base or mold. Tearing rather than cutting the paper means that it will have rough edges which will give a smoother surface than straight edges when glued down in layers. Paper may be torn against a ruler to make fairly uniform strips.

Another method, called lamination, consists of gluing together several sheets of paper to make one strong flexible sheet. This can then be shaped over a base or cut into strips before it is applied.

The third method involves breaking down small pieces of paper into a mash or pulp by soaking them in water for several hours. The water is then squeezed out of the paper until it becomes a pulp, and glue is added to make it bind together. Paper mash is often used to add texture and strength to an object molded from strips of papier mâché, but can also be molded like clay.

There are several commercial mixes available for making 'instant' paper mash, to which only water has to be added. These are easy to use and can be bought from art and craft suppliers.

Modeling on plasticine

Plasticine is the simplest of flexible molds to use, since it is easy to model quite a complex shape which will also stay firm while the papier mâché is applied to it.

The charming papier mâché birds and animals shown on these pages are not at all difficult to make, using the most common and also the simplest method of applying the paper—the strip method.

You will need:

Plasticine (about 453gm (1 lb) for an animal or bird 7.5cm (3″) high).

Newspaper or magazine paper, and soft tissues.

Epoxy resin glue, or a commercial wallpaper paste, or flour-and-water paste, or liquid starch to which two tablespoons of salt or sand are added per liter (quart) for extra strength.®

Vaseline.®

Kitchen knife, waxed paper, coarse and fine sandpaper.

White emulsion paint.

Brushes and poster or acrylic paints.

Two 2.5cm (1″) household paintbrushes.

Glass eyes (those used in soft toy making are suitable).

General-purpose glue.

Small bell (for the cat).

12.5cm (5″) length of thin string (from which to hang the cat's bell).

Lengths of raffia measuring about 8.5m (9yd) long altogether, for the large hen's nest.

Clear plasticized varnish.

☐ Mold the shape of the animal or bird in plasticine, omitting details such as beaks and ears. Keep the basic shapes simple and sloping gently out toward the base, without undercuts, so that the plasticine is easily removed when the papier mâché is hard. Smooth the plasticine, using a knife or a ruler if necessary.

☐ Place the mold on a sheet of waxed paper and coat the mold with Vaseline. This prevents the papier mâché from sticking to the mold.

☐ Tear newspaper or magazine paper into very small pieces, not more than about 2.5cm x 1.25cm (1″x ½″), and smaller still for the neck and tail areas.

☐ Moisten each piece with a small amount of the prepared glue or paste and place it on the mold. (Adhesives should be applied sparingly so that the pieces will dry quickly and evenly.) Each piece should slightly overlap the previous one. When the entire mold is covered in this way, smooth the paper

down with a household paintbrush and fingers making sure there are no gaps.

☐ Repeat until about eight coats of paper have been applied, except when covering the small cat's mold. In order to fix the bell on the cat, cover this mold with the first four or five layers of paper only, then thread the bell on to a length of string. Tie the string around the neck of the cat over the paper layers, with the bell in position in the front. Cover the mold with the last three or four layers of paper so that the surface is smooth and the string does not show as a ridge in the paper. It is a good idea to use paper of different colors or types for different coats, to help check that each layer is completely and evenly covered.

☐ Model the beak, ears and other details on the covered molds with shredded soft tissues mixed with paste or glue.

☐ Set the model aside to dry in a warm place such as on a sunny windowsill, near a radiator, or out in the sun, keeping it on the sheet of waxed paper. Allow the model to dry for at least a day.

☐ With the tip of a kitchen knife, ease out the plasticine. This is a great deal easier to do if the knife is warm.

Note: you could also remove the mold by sawing all around the model and removing the laminated cast in two halves. The two halves, however, would then have to be stuck together again with two or three more layers of paper, which would take much longer.

☐ Any rough edges on the model should now be sanded lightly with coarse and then fine sandpaper, until smooth.

☐ You could apply a layer of epoxy resin to the model, for extra strength.

☐ Apply two coats of white emulsion paint to the model with a household paintbrush. This gives a uniformly colored surface to decorate.

☐ When the paint is dry, apply general-

To make the large cat, model the shape in plasticine over a base of boxes, to avoid using a huge amount of plasticine. When you are satisfied with the shape, moisten the paper strips with glue or paste and stick down.

the score lines with a knife to remove the two halves from the mold. Stick them together again with more damp papier mâché, at the same time applying it to any cracks or bumps.

☐ Let this dry—if it is put in a warm oven with the door open at this stage (110°C or 225°F), it will quickly dry out and become very hard indeed. Sand down, paint and finish as for the first method described.

Mixed instant papier mâché can be stored in a plastic bag in a refrigerator for about a week.

This cat, like the larger cat behind it (designed by Lorraine Johnson), makes a charming shelf decoration.

purpose glue to the backs of the glass eyes and stick them in position.

☐ With the large watercolor brush, paint the background color of the animal or bird with poster or acrylic paint. With the smaller brush, paint features, spots, feathers, whiskers, or whatever you think is suitable or amusing.

☐ When the paint is dry, apply two coats of clear plasticized varnish to the object.

☐ For the larger hen's nest, braid the lengths of raffia and sew them together with smaller pieces of raffia into a nest shape.

Using instant papier mâché. For an easier and quicker way to make a bird or animal like those illustrated, use instant papier mâché, which is a pulp. As well as the materials already described, you will need two plastic bags, a rolling pin or milk bottle, and commercial instant paper pulp such as that sold by hobby shops.

☐ Make up the papier mâché according to the manufacturer's directions.

☐ Mold the plasticine as described and coat with Vaseline.®

☐ Roll out the instant papier mâché between two plastic bags to a thickness of 6mm (¼").

☐ Remove the top bag and, keeping the rolled-out papier mâché on the bag below it, apply to the mold, smoothing down around the mold with the plastic bag. Remove the bag and smooth the papier mâché into its final shape with a damp knife.

☐ While the papier mâché is still damp, score a line with the knife around the center of the model, dividing it into two identical halves. Note: removing the cast in two pieces and joining them again can be done easily with instant paper pulp. Do not remove the cast from the mold at this stage.

☐ Set aside the model to dry. Instant papier mâché will dry at room tempera-

ture but for faster drying, put it in a warm place as described for conventional papier mâché.

☐ When the model is dry, cut along

Melvin Grey

Introducing topiary art

Topiary art dates from Roman times or even earlier. It involves clipping bushes to represent other objects. Thus a hedge is an elementary form of topiary art, since it is basically a row of bushes clipped to represent a wall. A simple hedge can be embellished with castellations, curves, or projecting buttresses and various finials.

Though topiary art seems to be a dying craft there are still many good examples of it in Virginia, and in Britain and France, some dating back to the early 17th century.

Occasionally by the roadside or in old gardens it is possible to see a fine specimen of a clipped yew tree, perhaps 3m (10′) high, which has been patiently shaped through several generations, each adding a further tier.

Classical topiary shapes include a cone, a ball, a standard (a ball-on-stem) or a cube. Beyond these shapes the only limits to topiary projects are your clipping skill, your powers of imagination and the limits of growth of your subject.

A corkscrew, spiral shape, ball-on-cube, cone-on-drum and other geometrical forms are also quite common, though animals, birds, people and objects of almost any description can be created.

Most of these shapes will only involve the use of one bush, but it is possible to incorporate a number of bushes into one design.

A large four-legged animal would require four bushes planted wide apart. The body, arms and head will gradually be formed by allowing the growths to extend, at the same time training them to the appropriate shape.

It is worth while before embarking on a topiary project to study carefully the characteristics of your bush. How high will it grow? How fast does it grow? How wide will it grow? What type of soil does it need in order to grow?

Any topiary work will take at least four years to reach anything like its true shape and bulk. Thus one of the main attributes of a topiarist must be patience.

Shrubs to use

Any fairly dense hedging shrub can be used for topiary art but English yew (*Taxus baccata*) and common boxwood (*Buxus sempervirens*) are the general favorites.

For simple geometrical designs including cones, pyramids, standards and spirals it is essential to have not only plants of uniform growth, but also ones which have a single stem or leader. It is then just a matter of clipping to shape, either on a long or short stem, merely reducing the radial shoots to the desired graded length. Annual clipping will make the topiary work dense and firm in outline.

For simple cone shapes, shrubs of upright, as opposed to outward, outline should be chosen, such as cypress (*Chamaecyparis lawsoniana* 'Fletcheri') or the Irish yew (*Taxus baccata* 'Fastigiata').

Prickly plants, though less pleasant to work with, are suitable for most topiary shapes. In fact European hawthorn (*Crataegus oxyacantha*) was one of the most ancient hedging and topiary subjects; Common Holly (*Ilex aquifolium*) can also be used.

For uniformity of shape in a formal

A fine old topiary garden at Antony House, Cornwall owned by the English National Trust. The yew 'wigwam' and hedge finial are at least 200 years old.

Graham Thomas

garden it is necessary to choose bushes that have been grown from cuttings of a similar type, or alternatively that have been raised from seed. It is astonishing the different growth rates of differently raised bushes.

Yellow variegated yews (*Taxus variegata lutea*), hollies (*Ilex aquifolium*) and golden privet (*Ligustrum ovalifolium 'Aureum'*) all grow at relatively uniform rates and are suitable for classic shapes in a formal garden.

Yew (*Taxus baccata*) is the best bush to use for large topiary projects, though hedging honeysuckle (*Lonicera nitida*) which grows abundantly is also useful, particularly when a more 'instant' result is required.

Clipping

A classical topiarist will only require a pair of shears and perhaps a step ladder to pursue his craft. Clipping is the only method he will use to shape a bush. It may well take a matter of years to create the desired shape and mistakes will prove hard to disguise. Beginners should exercise a good deal of caution. Clip only small amounts at a time, start at the top and work down, repeatedly standing back from your work and surveying it.

Cones are a simple shape with which to begin. A good guide for a beginner is to use two sticks of equal length tied together at one end to form a long

V-shape, which is then placed over the bush to check for shape while clipping (fig.1).

Paul Williams

1. *Sticks used as an aid to cutting.*

Beginners should avoid topiary work of a spherical shape, unless the bush to be clipped grows abundantly and in this way quickly camouflages any bad errors. It is only with experience that the topiarist can achieve a uniform sphere. Practice clipping spheres using bushes in unimportant areas of the garden.

'Instant' topiary work

Though the classical topiarist would throw up his hands in horror at this topiary form, it is in fact probably more practical than the old style in our fast-moving modern society. People move house frequently, and few are going to want to put years of labor

Formal shaped common box at Lytes Cary, Somerset, England.

into something that will never be appreciated by them or their families. As growth is a secondary factor for 'instant' topiary work, it does mean that today's family can appreciate the fruits of their labor.

'Instant' topiary art involves shaping an existing, free-grown bush with artificial aids. Canes and wires are used to tie down branches and train the bush into shape. Unwanted branches are removed.

The topiary shape can usually be gauged, using some imagination, by bending branches and looking into the shape of the bush. Bushes of irregular shape, perhaps with several main shoots projecting, lend themselves to fantasies of all kinds.

You will need:
Stout sticks of various lengths, according to the size of the specimen. Galvanized wire, about 3-4mm ($\frac{1}{10}''$-$\frac{1}{8}''$). Thin galvanized wire, string or 'Twist-it' ties.
Crow-bar for making holes for sticks.
Wire cutters.
Scissors.
Pruning shears.
Pruning saw for large branches.
Garden shears.
Step ladder for high bushes.
Trestles and planks for very large specimens.

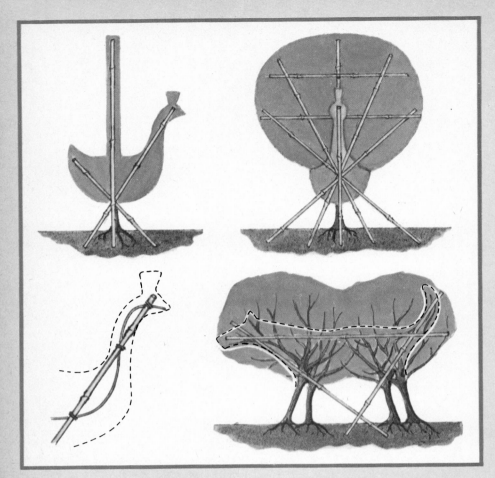

2. *Bushes can be shaped by artificial means. Sticks are inserted through the bush and into the ground and the bush is trained using galvanized wire.*

branches and these aids, growths can be made to descend (which is not possible with classical topiary work). However it is important that the entire descending length is created in one operation. It is a difficult job to extend the length downward in years to come, since all growth normally extends upward and outward.

After tying all the main branches and any others essential to your design into suitable positions onto sticks, attend to the wayward shoots. Tie these into position wherever possible. All that remains to be done is to clip the bush to its final design.

The bush should now be clipped to shape twice annually for the first two years, after which an annual clipping will suffice.

Caring for topiary work

Given a good start and fertile soil, an 'instant' topiary project should have considerable effect after three or four years.

As with hedges and all forms of clipping, really close shearing is essential once the outline has been made. Even with close clipping the design inevitably grows larger very gradually. This is the reason for the clumsy and grotesque shapes seen in old gardens, where often the original conception has been lost, legs widen, beaks turn into snouts and necks and ears completely disappear!

In the earlier stages it is wise to tie into position of clip away all shoots extraneous to the design as they

Decide on your shape. It is necessary to start with a well-established bush, growing strongly with plenty of supple young branches. Old stiff wood is insufficiently pliable to be of use. Position your sticks (fig.2). The stakes or the poles need to be inserted firmly in the ground; their lengths can be adjusted after the design is completed.

Tie the branches into the desired position. The strain will relax once the branches have adjusted themselves to their new positions.

Crossed sticks can be used for training flat surfaces, such as the expanded tail of a peacock (see fig.2). Stout galvanized wire can be tied to sticks for curved necks and arms. With pliant

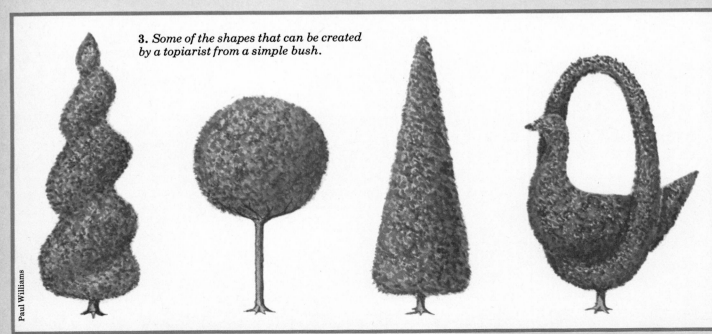

3. *Some of the shapes that can be created by a topiarist from a simple bush.*

Graham Thomas

grow. The best time for the annual clipping is in late summer, or early autumn, depending on how long you can tolerate a shaggy appearance. The summer's growth will then be completed and the topiary work is made tidy for another season.

Clipping of any kind, particularly with evergreens, reduces the leaf surface.

This obviously weakens the shrub, thus, to aid its good health, all hedges and topiary designs which are old and established should be given an annual application of a balanced fertilizer in early summer.

In due course the ends of the sticks will rot and can then be pulled out of the bush. The stout galvanized wire

Peacocks as finials to hedges at Hidcote, Gloucestershire, England.

can be left permanently inside the specimens however, as it will not show. String or thin wire which is needed to tie in the smaller growths must be removed after two years since the ties will eventually throttle the twigs.

Picture making with macramé

Yarn —
macramé 9

Picture making is an unusual aspect of macramé and is also the aspect which requires the most ingenuity and experimentation.

Macramé pictures are a development of the technique used for wall hangings (Macramé chapter 6, page 1046) in that several shapes are composed in macramé and then stuck in position on a flat background to make a picture.

Designing

Choose shapes which are distinctive and easy to draw. Trees are a good choice because the texture of the macramé resembles a tree's trunk and branches. Houses, ships and many animals are suitable subjects because they have shapes which are recognizable by outline and do not need elaborate detail. People are less easy to depict unless in costume such as a clown's or sailor's.

Three-dimensional effects. Simple features can be introduced by the use of beads and it is possible to add a three-dimensional effect by working parts of the macramé around a firm foundation. This is mainly suitable for rows of cording worked around a core of wood or bamboo instead of string.

A clever example of this is shown in the town scene—the trees are knotted over bamboo. Separate fine pieces are used for each branch and, as two branches meet, the pieces are held together and the knots worked over both of them. As the branches meet the trunk, all the lengths of bamboo are held together to make a thicker core.

The knots. Choose knots which help form the shapes or the character of the picture. Double cording knots, for example, can be used for close firm areas; diagonal cording can be worked for leaf shapes and angles. Alternating flat knots are good for covering a large area quickly and for curves (Macramé chapter 2, page 204). Braids of flat knots can give an impression of stripes (Macramé chapter 4, page 594).

The background. This can be hardboard, plywood or even chipboard or cork. You could paint the background or you could cover it with fabric.

Working the design. Draw the individual shapes to the desired size on paper and pin the paper to your macramé board so that you can work over the paper shape. As you complete each shape, place it in position on the background but do not glue down until you have placed on all the shapes and can judge the full effect. Use a clear general-purpose adhesive to stick the shapes to the background.

Right: knotting a sailor's figure to add to a macramé boat picture. Designs by Germaine Brotherton.

Below: town scene is given extra dimension by knotting trees around bamboo.

Alasdair Ogilvie

Wardrobe for a Victorian doll

In Toys chapter 11, page 2178, patterns and directions are given for a Victorian doll's body. This chapter describes how to make the doll's wardrobe.

These clothes can be made very cheaply, particularly if you already have scraps of suitable fabrics and trimmings. Be sure to use tiny beads and fine lace for decoration, as too heavy a trim will spoil the proportions. If you have had to adapt the body pattern to suit the doll's head, make sure that you alter the clothes patterns likewise. The patterns are designed to fit the body perfectly, but you should check the fit of the clothes on the doll as you work, as you would if making your own clothes. As the clothes are all tight fitting, it is particularly important to obtain the correct fit.

Adapt the patterns given here and use your imagination to create an entire wardrobe for your doll.

Make paper patterns for all the clothes using the graph patterns (pages 2198-99). Allow an extra 6mm ($\frac{1}{4}''$) for seams all around.

Melvin Grey

The boots

You will need:

30cm (12″) by 30cm (12″) of felt, suede or soft leather.
Matching thread.
Fabric adhesive.
Approximately 50 small beads.
Contrasting silk embroidery thread.

☐ Cut boots, soles and heels out of fabric. No seam allowance is needed on soles and heels. With right sides facing, machine stitch back seams. Turn right side out.

☐ Wrap the boots around the legs and turn in the front edges by 6mm (¼″) so that they meet edge to edge. Catch stitch neatly in place.

☐ Glue the soles into position, sticking them to the soles of the doll's feet and the inside edges of the boots.

☐ Glue the heels in place.

☐ For a firm, neat finish, work running stitch around the outer edges of the soles and heels.

☐ Sew small beads in pairs at approximately 10mm (⅜″) intervals to each side of the front join.

☐ Using contrasting embroidery thread, sew cross stitches down the front of the boots so that the point of each cross coincides with a bead, to suggest lacing.

The corselet

You will need:

40cm (16″) by 18cm (7″) of pink, white or flesh-colored cotton fabric.
Matching thread.
6 snaps or hooks and eyes.
Narrow lace trimming.

☐ Cut out the four pieces for the corselet from fabric.

☐ With right sides facing, stitch the four pieces together at side and back seams.

☐ Finish the front edges by turning in 6mm (¼″) and machine stitching.

☐ Fasten the front overlap with snaps or hooks and eyes.

☐ Add narrow lace for shoulder straps.

☐ Trim the front and bottom edges with narrow lace.

The pantaloons

You will need:

91cm (36″) by 60cm (24″) of cotton fabric. This quantity is sufficient to make a matching petticoat.
Matching thread.
Narrow elastic for the waist.
Lace trimming.

☐ Cut out the two pieces for the pantaloons from fabric.

☐ With right sides facing, machine stitch the center seams.

☐ Fold right sides together, so center front seam lies on center back seam, and machine stitch the inner leg seams.

☐ Hem the waist edge and thread elastic through. Turn right side out.

☐ Add lace trim to the leg bottoms.

The petticoat

You will need:

Cotton fabric to match the pantaloons —see fabric requirements above.
Matching thread.
Narrow elastic for the waist.
Lace trimming.

☐ Cut the four petticoat pieces out of fabric.

☐ With right sides facing, machine stitch the four panels together.

☐ Hem the waist edge and thread narrow elastic through.

☐ Sew lace trimming to bottom edge.

Delightful wardrobe for a Victorian doll, designed by Audrey Barker.

Paul Kemp

Careful use of trimming is important.

The dress

You will need:

1.8m (2yd) of 90cm (36″) wide fine fabric such as calico or silk, or 1.4m (1½yd) of 90cm (36″) wide heavy-weight fabric such as tweed for the skirt and bodice. If you use a fine fabric, cut four skirt panels from the paper pattern. If you use a heavy-weight fabric only cut three panels. This will result in a less full skirt, but the waist would otherwise be too bulky when gathered into the bodice. The quantities given are sufficient to make the matching bonnet.
Matching thread.
Light-weight fabric such as silk or fine cotton to line bodice.
Assorted lace trimming.
4 snaps or hooks and eyes.
Narrow elastic for sleeves.
Tiny beads for decoration.

The Victorian style of dress consists of a very tightly fitting bodice with full skirt and sleeves.

☐ Cut out the bodice, sleeves and skirt panels from dress fabric. Also cut bodice from lining fabric.

☐ With right sides facing, stitch both bodice and lining at side and shoulder seams.

☐ Sew lace trimming to bodice.

☐ Place lining to bodice, right sides facing and seams matching, and stitch along back edges and neck edge. Turn right side out and tack lining to bodice around armholes and waist edges.

☐ Fasten back overlap with snaps or hooks and eyes.

☐ Sew lace trimming to the sleeves as illustrated.

☐ With right sides facing, stitch inner arm seams.

☐ Hem the sleeve edges and thread elastic through for a gathered effect.

☐ Sew sleeve to bodice by sewing armhole seams by hand, with right sides facing, and working bodice and lining together as one.

☐ Stitch the skirt panels together, right sides facing, leaving open a small section of the top of one seam. This

2197

will be the back seam. Turn right side out.

☐ Sew lace trimming to skirt near the bottom.

☐ Gather the top of the skirt with running stitch, and sew skirt to bodice by hand, with right sides facing and again working bodice and lining together.

☐ Make a small neat hem around the bottom of the skirt.

The bonnet

You will need:

Fabric to match dress—see fabric requirements for dress.

Matching thread.

Fine fabric for lining. A smart co-ordinated effect is obtained by using the same fabric as for the petticoat and pantaloons.

Paper or buckram for stiffening.

Assorted lace trimming to match dress.

Ribbon for tying bonnet under doll's chin.

☐ Cut out a circular back section of the bonnet from dress fabric and lining.

☐ Cut a brim piece out of dress fabric and lining. Also cut a brim piece without seam allowance from stiffening.

☐ Place the two brim pieces together, right sides facing, and stitch around the curved ends and longer side leaving the section between points A and B open.

☐ Turn right side out and insert stiffening.

☐ Place the two back sections together, right sides facing, and stitch around the edge, leaving a gap through which to turn fabric.

☐ Turn right side out and slip-stitch opening.

☐ Work gathering stitches with a double thread around the edge of the circular back section, close to the edge.

☐ With right sides facing, stitch the top fabric of brim between points A and B to the back section.

☐ Turn in the seam allowance on the lining of the brim and slip-stitch in place.

☐ Draw up the gathering threads on the back section so that the bonnet fits the doll's head, and fasten the loose ends.

☐ Sew ribbons high up on each side of the inside of the brim. If they are too low, they will pull the brim down when tied under the doll's chin.

☐ Sew a lace frill to the back section of the bonnet where it is not attached to the brim.

☐ Sew an abundance of assorted lace trimming to match the dress to cover brim as illustrated.

☐ To make ear rosettes, gather up two small lengths of fabric or ribbon to form two flower shapes and sew one to each end of brim.

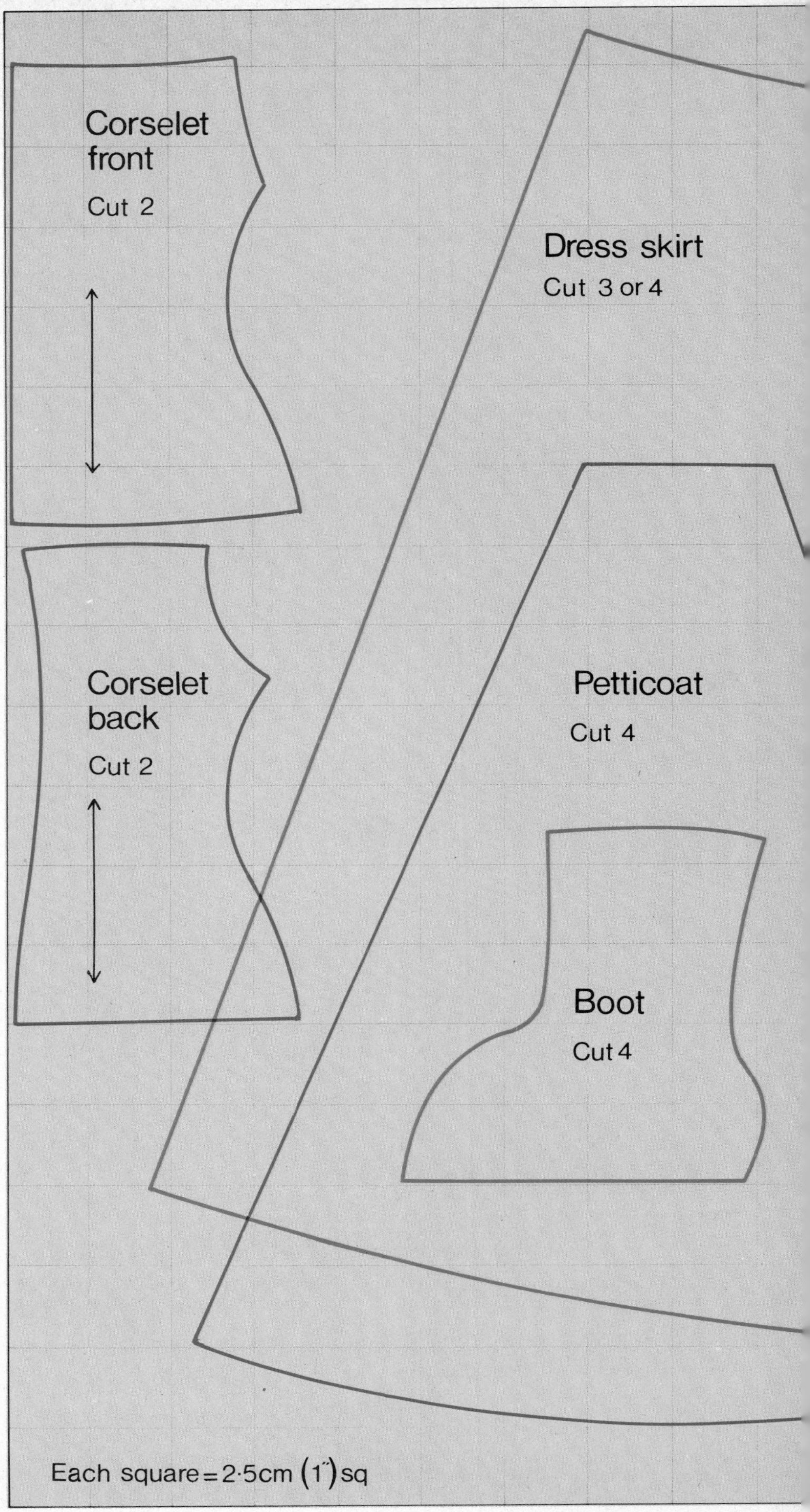

Corselet front

Cut 2

Dress skirt

Cut 3 or 4

Corselet back

Cut 2

Petticoat

Cut 4

Boot

Cut 4

Each square = 2·5cm (1″) sq

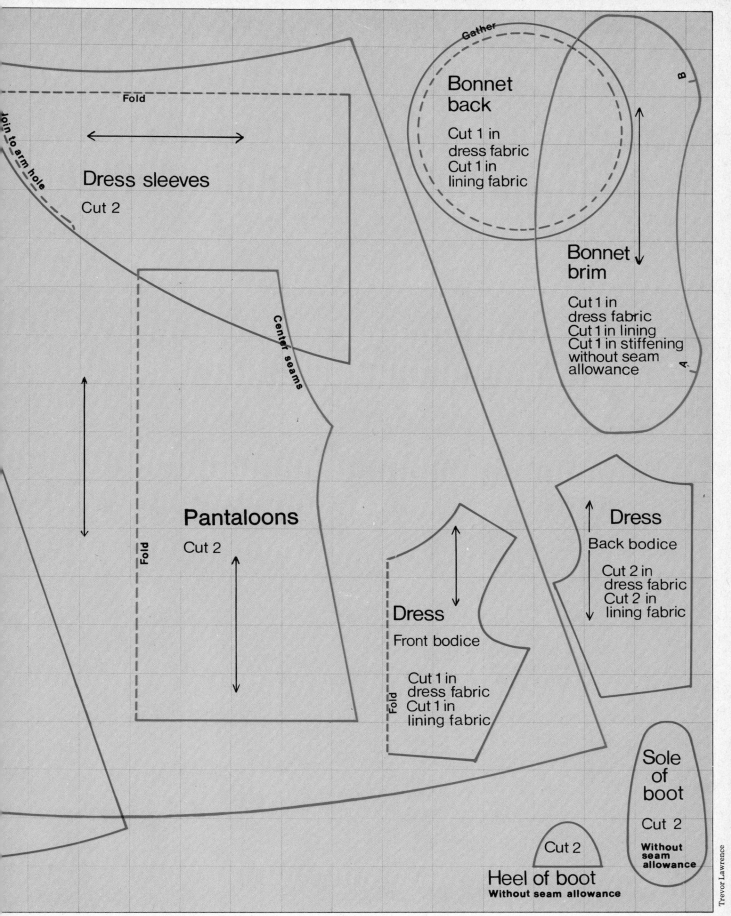

Gather

Bonnet back

Cut 1 in dress fabric
Cut 1 in lining fabric

B

Fold

Join to arm hole

Dress sleeves

Cut 2

Center seams

Bonnet brim

Cut 1 in dress fabric
Cut 1 in lining
Cut 1 in stiffening without seam allowance

A

Pantaloons

Cut 2

Fold

Fold

Dress

Front bodice

Cut 1 in dress fabric
Cut 1 in lining fabric

Dress

Back bodice

Cut 2 in dress fabric
Cut 2 in lining fabric

Sole of boot

Cut 2

Without seam allowance

Cut 2

Heel of boot

Without seam allowance

Trevor Lawrence

The art of 'champlevé'

Champlevé, or inlaid enameling, is the technique in which depressions are hollowed out of the metal surface and these are then filled with enamel. For many hundreds of years *champlevé* was one of the main techniques of the enameler's craft. It is not widely practiced today, however, which is a pity because it is comparatively easy. Moreover, it is a technique which cannot be mistaken for anything other than what it is—enameling on metal, ie both enamel and metal can be easily seen in the finished work. In this respect it is similar to its sister technique, *cloisonné*. *Champlevé* is, however, quicker to execute and is more suitable for large panels and plaques. It is also more durable than *cloisonné*. After the decline of the Byzantine *cloisonné* workshops the center of enameling moved to Western Europe where, for the next three hundred years (1200-1500AD), *champlevé* was almost the only type of enameling produced. It was made in such large quantities that thousands of *champlevé* artifacts still exist and can be seen in all the prominent museums of the world.

The metal
Copper is suitable for *champlevé* work. The copper used should be no thinner than 1.25mm (16-18 gauge). The copper must be thoroughly cleaned on both sides with steel wool and scouring powder. Once the metal has been

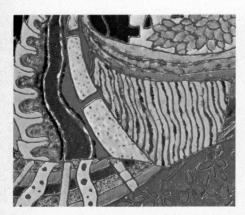

Melvin Grey

cleaned take care not to get finger grease on it as this will stop the resist used on the areas of the metal not to be etched from adhering properly to the copper.

Hollowing out metal

In medieval times hammer, chisel and gouge were the tools used for hollowing out the metal. Today this hard work has been replaced by an acid bath.

Nitric acid is most commonly used as the etching medium. It can be bought as a liquid concentrate. For very fine work however, use ferric chloride.

Nitric acid. To make an acid bath using nitric acid, add one part nitric acid to three parts water. In an acid-proof container (plastic or glass) large enough to accommodate easily the piece to be etched, make up enough of the acid solution to cover the piece by about 1.5cm ($\frac{1}{2}$″).

It takes about five hours for this nitric acid solution to eat down to half the thickness of 1.25mm (16-18 gauge) copper.

Warning: great care must be taken when dealing with nitric acid—if it touches the skin it will burn and it gives off poisonous fumes. When preparing an acid bath with nitric acid *always* pour the acid into the water. Never pour the water into the acid as this will cause dangerous splashing.

Country landscape designed by Richard Casey is made from two panels of copper mounted together to make a 'champlevé' picture 40cm x 22.5cm (14″ x 9″). The small photographs are close-up details of the piece.

Always wear rubber gloves and, to avoid inhaling the poisonous fumes, *never* stoop over the acid bath longer than is strictly necessary. For the same reason, use a container with a lid for the acid bath, such as an old oven-proof glass casserole, or any other suitable glass container.

Work in a well-ventilated room or workshop.

Dispose of the acid bath, preferably when it has become weakened or 'tired' from etching copper. (Tired nitric acid becomes very blue in color.) Turn on the cold water faucet and let it run while you pour the acid bath slowly and carefully down the sink. Leave the faucet running for about ten minutes after pouring away acid. (This method is not suitable for disposing of large quantities of acid.)

Ferric chloride does not require such great care in handling as does nitric acid—if ferric chloride touches the skin it will merely stain, it does not give off poisonous fumes and does not splash. Ferric chloride is obtainable in lump form. To make an acid bath, the lumps should be crushed to a rough powder with a knife or spoon and mixed with an equal quantity of water. An old jam jar is useful for this.

To be etched with ferric chloride, a piece of copper must be turned face down in the acid bath with matchsticks placed under it to keep the metal off the floor of the container (fig.1). It takes about seven or eight hours for ferric chloride to etch 1.25mm (16-18 gauge) copper.

The resist. The areas of the metal which are not to be etched must be

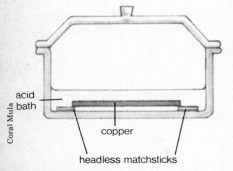

1. *Headless matchsticks are positioned under the metal to allow acid to flow underneath the metal.*

protected with a layer of acid-resistant paint or varnish—called a resist.

The stopping-out varnish sold by craft suppliers for etching is a suitable resist. Alternatively the bitumen paint used to paint outdoor wrought iron objects is quite satisfactory.

As the acid will attack any exposed metal, no matter how small the area, you must be very careful to cover with the resist all parts of the metal you have planned to leave exposed in the completed work.

You must also protect the edges and back of the piece. This can be done with melted candle wax, painted on with a brush.

The design

Keep your designs simple and bold initially until you are better acquainted with the time and process of the 'biting' function of the acid.

The blue dish

Although the directions given here are for making the dish in the photograph the method can be applied to such items as copper panels and pieces of jewelry.

You will need:
Equipment. 3 acid-proof containers

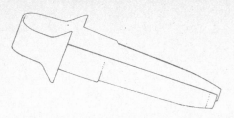

2. *Plastic forceps like these can be used to put the work into the acid bath and to remove it from the acid bath.*

with lids (plastic or glass).
Plastic tongs, tweezers or the plastic print forceps sold by photographic suppliers (fig.2).
Craft knife.
Rubber gloves.
Feather or wooden spoon.
Old knife.
Old nail brush.
Enameling equipment as described in Enamel chapter 1, page 106, plus a stilt.
Materials. 1.25mm (16-18 gauge) almost flat copper dish, 10cm (4″) in diameter.
Nitric acid.
Resist, as previously described.
Melted candle wax.
1 teaspoonful gum arabic mixed with 0.28 liters (1¼ cups) distilled water.
Brushes for applying resist, candle wax and gum arabic solution when counter enameling.
Turpentine.
Opaque enamels in chosen colors.

Counter enameling powder.
Carborundum® stone.
Steel wool and scouring powder.
Fine steel wool and liquid detergent.
Tracing paper, hard pencil and carbon paper.
Metal polish or the clear lacquer sold by art suppliers for lacquering oil paintings.
Soft cloths.

☐ Cut the tracing paper and carbon paper to fit the dish.
☐ Remove paper from dish and clean copper thoroughly with steel wool and scouring powder. Then rinse and dry with soft cloth.
☐ Trace design from the photograph below, place carbon paper and tracing back onto dish and, with a hard pencil, transfer the design onto the metal.
☐ Paint the resist on all of the areas which are to be left exposed in the completed work.
Note: take care not to get any finger grease on the metal while transferring the design or painting on the resist or the resist will not adhere satisfactorily to the copper.
☐ Leave the resist to dry completely if using stopping-out varnish or until almost dry if using bitumen paint (about 2 hours).
☐ Have a final look at the design and correct any flaws with a craft knife.
☐ Protect the edge and back of the dish

The finished dish, shown full size. Use this as a tracing pattern for the design.

by painting on melted wax. Allow wax and resist to dry.

☐ Put on rubber gloves and prepare the acid bath, remembering to add the acid to the water and not vice versa.

☐ Place dish gently in the acid bath, right way up, using plastic forceps.

☐ Leave the acid to work, checking occasionally to see how the etching is progressing and to give the acid a gentle stir with a feather or spoon. After about three hours the acid solution will have lost some of its strength. Make up a new acid bath in the same way as before and then, using plastic forceps, transfer dish to it.

☐ When the acid has eaten down to half the thickness of the copper (this takes about five hours), remove dish from the bath with plastic forceps. (Do not throw away acid bath yet.)

☐ Wash the dish under hot running water. This will also remove the wax.

☐ Remove the resist by scraping it off with an old knife, while still under the hot, running water. The resist will have been softened by the acid and should come off fairly easily. Remove last traces of resist with turpentine and a soft cloth.

This 'champlevé' hair ornament shows a good combination of exposed metal and enamel. Designed by Horatio Goni.

☐ Clean the piece again under the hot, running water, using scouring powder and steel wool. Rinse thoroughly and dry with a soft cloth.

The piece can now be enameled. The design originally drawn on the metal with the resist will appear in relief.

☐ Switch on the kiln so that it will be hot enough, ie bright orange, by the time you are ready to enamel.

☐ Paint the back of the dish with gum arabic solution and sift on counter enameling powder (Enamel chapter 5, page 514).

☐ Pick up the piece by the edges, without disturbing the counter enameling powder. Turn the dish right way up and place it carefully on the stilt.

☐ Fill the cells on the right side of the dish with enamel, leaving the relief parts to serve as walls to contain the areas of color. Use the wet pack method (Enamel chapter 7, page 996), ie mix enamel to a paste with gum arabic solution.

☐ Be sure to pack plenty of enamel

inside the cells for this layer of enamel will sink to about half its depth when fired, necessitating another layer of enamel of the same color as the first.

☐ Place stilt on the wire mesh stand and dry out the enamel thoroughly on top of the kiln before firing.

☐ Fire the piece. Refill the cells, dry as before and re-fire.

☐ After this second firing, you will probably find that the enamel projects a little above the metal design. The work must be smoothed down with Carborundum® until enamel and metal are level.

☐ Wash the work under the faucet, using a nail brush to remove any traces of grit left from the smoothing process. Re-fire to bring back the sheen to the enamels. The exposed copper parts of the design will now be black with fire-scale.

☐ In another acid-proof container make up a solution by adding one part of the acid bath left over from the etching process to ten parts of water. (Tired acid becomes very blue in color.)

☐ To loosen the fire-scale from the exposed copper on the dish, place the work in this weak acid bath. (A weak acid bath is used so that the enamel does not get attacked by too strong acid.)

☐ Leave dish in the weak acid bath for between half an hour and an hour (checking after half an hour to see if fire-scale has loosened sufficiently). Then remove dish with plastic forceps and wash carefully under running water, using very fine steel wool and liquid detergent. Do not use scouring powder or a rough grade of steel wool which would damage the surface of the enamel.

☐ Polish the piece all over with metal polish and a soft cloth to bring up the sheen of the copper.

Alternatively, lacquer over the metal parts only.

This double-headed sea serpent pendant was designed by Horatio Goni.

How to make beeswax polish

Bees were probably one of the first animals kept by man and over the centuries provided many of the necessaries of man's existence: honey for food and medicine; mead for wine; wax to dip candles, fill cracks in the roof and polish tables and chairs. Today, honey is still widely available but beeswax, like many other natural products, has become expensive and is considered a luxury item.

This is largely due to the development of synthetics which, though less expensive, do not necessarily improve on the natural products. Luckily, in the case of beeswax, the old, time-honored recipes are still with us and, although the materials are not cheap, the resulting polish is a superior product and the cost is less than the same type of polish bought in a store.

What is beeswax?

Bees make honey and wax. Under their tiny bodies are eight wax glands. When they need to build their waxen honeycomb, they eat honey and hang together in long chains, making a living curtain with their bodies. They produce heat and liquid wax forms in the glands. As it comes into contact with air this solidifies into minute, delicate wafers like fish scales. The bees pick these up with their back legs and transfer them to their front legs, where the wax is held against the jaw. Using their mandibles like a bricklayer's trowel, bees construct cells to provide cradles for their larvae and store chambers for their pollen and honey. The resulting comb, melted down and cast into blocks, is the raw material of beeswax polish.

Beeswax melts at 63°-65°C (147°-150°F) so is one of the harder waxes, and it is the best wax by far for making polish. It gives a soft flat sheen to furniture and floors and has only one slight disadvantage: it is a little sticky.

To give a more reflective gloss to your polished surface you will need to add to beeswax a small amount of another natural wax—a technique which is also discussed in this chapter. The added wax, called carnauba wax is a vegetable wax from the wax palm tree; it makes beeswax polish less sticky.

The solvent

Beeswax is fairly hard and in order that it can be spread over a surface it has to be softened. This is done by using a solvent to render it into a more liquid form. The traditional solvent for beeswax is turpentine which not only has a pungent, clean smell but also brings out the aroma of the beeswax.

Beeswax polish is ideal for fine and antique furniture. To obtain extra gloss carnauba wax is added.

Liz Whiting

Graham Hogben

There is no substitute for beeswax, but mineral spirits is a satisfactory turpentine substitute, though it lacks the scent. This can be remedied by using half turpentine and half mineral spirits. The solvent will evaporate and leave just wax on the wood surface. Two types of polish—paste and emulsion—can be made easily in an ordinary kitchen.

Paste polish

This is simply a blend of wax with suitable solvent. When the resultant paste is spread lightly over furniture, the solvent evaporates and leaves a thin film of wax behind.

You will need:
Double boiler.
Saucepan with pouring lip.
A cooking thermometer.
A rotary beater or electric mixer.
A stove or hot plate (If you use a gas ring, an asbestos mat is recommended).
A graduated jug marked in milliliters (or pints).
Clean dry tobacco tins.
100gm (4oz) beeswax (available from most drugstores, or contact your nearest local beekeeper's association).
250ml (1¼ cups) mineral spirits or turpentine or a mixture of the two.

☐ Heat the wax in a double boiler until it melts.
☐ Raise the temperature to about 70°C (160°F).
☐ Place turpentine and/or mineral spirits into a small saucepan with a pouring lip and raise the temperature to 70°C (160°F).
☐ Maintaining both liquids at the same temperature, slowly pour the

Beeswax comes in a variety of shades of brown and many different textures.

solvent into the wax, beating the two thoroughly together with the hand beater or electric mixer.

Beeswax polish can be made at home quite quickly and does not require any specialist equipment.

Graham Hogben

Filling the tins. Your polish will give more pleasure if it presents an unblemished, smooth surface when you open a new tin.

Tobacco tins are useful for packing paste polish. Wash the tin in hot, soapy water and dry it off in a cool oven. This removes the tobacco smell.

☐ Pour close to the edges of the tin to prevent surface bubbles.

☐ Try to avoid a draft as folds or wrinkles may appear.

☐ Do not put on the lid until the polish is cold.

☐ Leave the tins undisturbed for several hours.

Emulsion polish

An emulsion is a liquid which contains oily or resinous particles in suspension. In the case of polish, emulsion consists of waxes and turpentine or mineral spirits (the wax element) suspended in water and soap (the water element).

For the wax element you will need:

125gm (4½oz) beeswax.

500ml (2½ cups) turpentine or mineral spirits or mixture of two.

For water element you will need:

13gm (½oz) pure soap flakes.

500ml (2½ cups) water.

A double boiler. Bottles and funnel. A stove or hot plate (if you use a gas ring, an asbestos mat is recommended). Cooking thermometer.

A rotary beater or electric mixer.

☐ Melt wax in a double boiler.

☐ Remove from stove and add the turpentine and/or mineral spirits.

☐ Return the mixture to the stove and heat it until the temperature reaches 80°C (180°F).

☐ In another pan with a pouring lip, mix soap flakes with boiling water and adjust temperature to 80°C (180°F). The same temperatures in the reacting substances produce the best emulsions.

☐ Using a hand beater slowly, or an electric mixer at its slowest speed begin to beat the wax mixture.

Very slowly pour the soap and water solution into the wax and continue beating for several minutes after a good emulsion forms.

To avoid lumps in emulsion polish add the soap solution slowly to the wax.

☐ Pour into clean, warmed bottles (using a funnel to avoid waste).

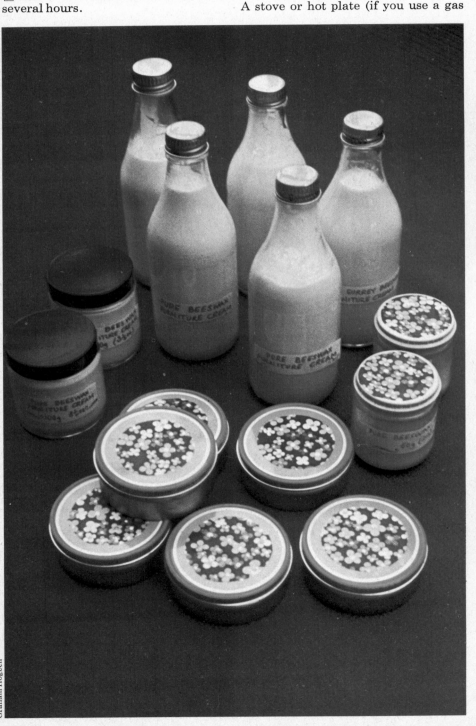

Above: the emulsion polish should be fluid enough to pour into bottles.

Left: non-returnable bottles and screw top tins and jars make good containers for emulsion and wax polish.

Graham Hogben

Carnauba wax

Carnauba wax comes from a palm tree in the Brazilian jungle. To protect its fronds from dehydration in the blazing tropical sun, the carnauba palm covers them with a protective coating of wax. A number of fronds may be cut each year without endangering the tree. They are laid out in rows to dry and turned several times. The wax begins to flake and then the fronds are threshed by beating with sticks so the wax falls off.

The carnauba wax flakes are melted over open fires and cast into rough blocks. Carnauba wax with a melting point of 83°-86°C (182°-188°F) gives great hardness and gloss to polishes. Carnauba has a country scent of newly mown hay.

Note: if adding carnauba wax to floor polish only use a small amount or your floor may be dangerously slippery.

Carnauba and beeswax polish

The method of making this paste polish is exactly the same as for the pure beeswax paste polish—you simply substitute a small amount of beeswax for carnauba wax.

You will need:

15gm ($\frac{1}{2}$oz) carbauba wax.
85gm ($3\frac{1}{2}$oz) beeswax.
500ml ($2\frac{1}{2}$ cups) solvent-turpentine, mineral spirits or a mixture.
Make polish as described previously.

Beeswax and carnauba wax emulsion is exactly the same as that for the beeswax emulsion, except temperatures can be raised to 90°C (195°F) and 25gm (1oz) of beeswax can be substituted for carnauba wax.

Variations

When you have made a few batches of polish you may wish to experiment and adapt the recipes to your own requirements. If you like a firmer polish reduce the proportion of solvent in the paste polish. Add extra solvent to emulsion polish and you will have a liquid wax polish (this is especially desirable for floors).

If you prefer a gloss finish on your furniture, increase the proportion of carnauba wax. Do not exceed 30% carnauba in your total wax or you may find it too hard a gloss.

Using the polish

Beeswax polish cleans and polishes the surface at one operation and is pleasant and easy to apply.

Apply a thin coat of polish, allow it to dry thoroughly, then buff with a duster.

Remember to use beeswax polish and emulsion sparingly. It is better to apply three or even four thin coats, polishing after each, than one thick one.

Repeat this process several times rather than trying to build up a thick coating of wax at one go.

All these polishes are particularly suitable for fine and antique furniture and they are also suitable for wood block floors or for polishing old fashioned linoleum. They are not suitable however for thermoplastic tiled floors and modern articles of furniture which have a synthetic spray finish (synthetic spray finishes should only be wiped with a damp duster or chamois). Ask a furniture salesman if in doubt.

Warning

Melted wax and wax solvents are flammable substances and should not be heated over a naked flame. Melt wax in a double boiler or a bowl standing in a pan of water.

If your wax should ignite do not attempt to extinguish the flame with water. Wax floats on water and your fire would spread over a wide area. Smother the flames with a large damp cloth, with sand or a foam fire extinguisher.

Carving and modeling

Carving and modeling leather involves cutting into the surface of a piece of leather and pressing down one side of the cut, so that one side is higher than the other, thereby creating a relief.

This technique is used to make all sorts of decorations on leather goods; it has even been used to draw portraits and landscapes, but looks at its best when the designs are kept simple.

Carved and modeled leather is used a lot in the western states, where the 'Western' style of carving and modeling, based on traditional designs used by the Spanish in South America to decorate their saddles, is particularly popular.

The leather used for carving and modeling should be the same type as for tooling, ie a vegetable-tanned russet hide with no lacquered or cellulose finish. The leather must be fairly thick, ie about 5mm ($\frac{3}{16}$"), unless the cuts are very shallow and the relief subtle. Before carving and modeling, the leather is moistened with a little water.

Tools
There are several types of tool used for this technique (see photo opposite).

A cutting or carving tool called a swivel knife, is used to make the cuts in the surface of the leather. This is a square-ended blade on a handle. The blade turns independently of the knife, hence its name, and is especially designed to enable curved as well as straight cuts to be made in the leather.

A beveler is wedge-shaped and is used to press the leather down on one side

Leather, decorated using carving and modeling techniques, dyed with aniline dyes, and then stitched together, to make a folder and blotter. Designed by John Williams.

of a cut to create a relief. It is held at 90° to the surface of the leather with the thicker side of the wedge shape (the toe) along the cut (fig.1), and the top is hit with a mallet or leather hammer.

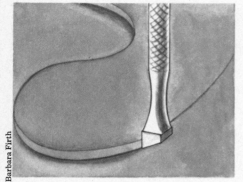

1. *The beveler is used to depress one side of a cut.*

Matting tools are similar to bevellers but have flat faces and are used to depress whole areas of a design. They can leave a smooth or textured surface on the leather depending on the face of the tool.

A deerfoot is used to smooth over curved areas of a design, and eliminate any unwanted marks caused by the beveling or matting tools.

Other tools are used to give specific textured effects such as the veiner which is used to add veins to leaves.

The design

Carving and modeling must be thought of in terms of three rather than two dimensions. It will be necessary to modify a simple line drawing before it can be transferred onto leather by carving and modeling. The lines in your design will represent the cuts that will be made in the leather. If you want a single raised line on the leather, it will be necessary to make a cut on each side of the line, leaving the area between the cuts raised. On paper, this raised line will be represented by two parallel lines, one for each cut. Be very careful when working out your design, and remember that each cut will divide a raised from a depressed area. Lightly shade in the areas that will be depressed.

When the design has been worked out, make a scale drawing of all the cutting lines on a sheet of paper, place the paper over the leather and draw over the lines with a pencil or ballpoint pen, thereby making a faint impression of the cutting lines on the leather.

Carving and modeling

When the design is lightly **marked** out, it can be carved and modeled into the leather.

Carving. The swivel knife is used to cut into the surface of the leather along the lines. To make it easier to cut into the leather the piece is first moistened with water. The cuts should be about half as deep as the thickness of the leather—if they are too deep the leather will be weakened. If you want some areas more in relief than others, vary the depth of cut. When cutting along straight lines, run the knife along the steel ruler. For curved lines, swivel the knife between thumb and third fingers as you cut (fig.2). The blade should always be at 90° to the leather and the cuts made toward you.

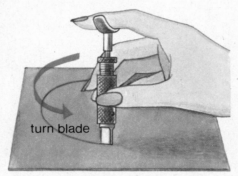

turn blade

2. *The blade of the swivel knife is turned as the cut is made.*

Your first attempts with the knife will obviously not be perfect, so practice on a scrap of leather until you can control the knife.

Modeling. The first part of the modeling process is to depress one side of each cut with the beveler. Consult your original drawing to make sure that you are depressing the correct side of the cut. When you have finished this there should be no cuts left which have not been pressed down on one side.

The next step is to go over the large areas which you want depressed with the matting tool. Some areas can be left as they are after the beveling tool has been used.

When you have finished using the matting tool, any unwanted lumps and bumps in the leather can be smoothed over with a deerfoot tool. Remember that the leather should be kept moist throughout the carving and modeling processes.

The folder

This folder can be used to hold writing pad and envelopes. It is decorated with carving and modeling and then dyed. The finished folder measures 41.6cm x 23cm (16¼″ x 9″) when open.

You will need:
Tools
Sharp leather-cutting knife.
Steel ruler.
Skiving knife.
Diamond stitching awl.
Harness needles.
Stitching clams or vise.
Edge shaver or medium grade sandpaper.
Dividers with adjustable screw.
Screw crease.
No. 6 thonging chisel.
Hammer or mallet.
Swivel knife.
Matting tool.
Beveler.
Deerfoot.

Materials
5mm ($\frac{3}{16}$″) thick vegetable-tanned russet cow-hide (ie leather that has not been given any cellulose or lacquered finish) 41.6cm x 25cm (16¼″ x 9¾″).
2mm ($\frac{1}{10}$″) thick vegetable-tanned russet cow-hide for the hinge of the folder 27cm x 6cm (10½″ x 2¼″).
Skiver to line the folder, 45cm x 25cm (18″ x 10″).
Linen thread.
Beeswax.
Leather dyes—powder or liquid.
Glue spreader.
Contact cement.
Sponge.
Triangle.
Pencils.
Sable brushes and piece of felt for applying dye.
Scrap of canvas.
Wax polish.
Polishing rags and brushes.
□ From the thick leather cut two rectangles 23cm x 19.5cm (9″ x 7⅝″), and four strips 1cm (⅜″) wide, two 41.6cm (16¼″) long and two 23cm (9″) long. Make sure all the corners are square.
□ Skive all along one longer edge of the back and front pieces on the flesh sides to a width of 1.5cm (⅝″) so that the leather tapers to a paper thin edge. These skived edges will be stitched on to the hinge, which is also skived down both longer edges on the flesh side to a width of 1.5cm (⅝″).

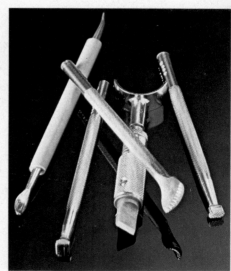

A selection of carving and modeling tools: deerfoot tool (left), beveler, swivel knife, veiner, matting tool.

Applying the design. Using the tracing pattern draw design on a sheet of paper or make up your own design. The central part of the design given here is applied to the front of the folder only. The back can be left plain or decorated with the border lines.

☐ Transfer the design onto the front of the folder on the grain side as described earlier.

☐ Damp the grain side of back and front with a little water on a sponge. First the border lines are tooled into the leather using the technique of cold tooling explained in Leather chapter 9, page 2118.

☐ Make the double lines around the back and front pieces using the screw crease.

☐ Run the screw crease against the steel ruler to obtain straight lines.

Next the central part of the design is carved and modeled into the leather.

☐ Using the swivel knife cut into the leather over the lines of the central design to form the diagonals, ovals and the rectangle containing them. The oval borders are made by cutting along the inner sections of each oval.

☐ Using the beveling tool, depress the side of each cut colored in blue and shaded blue on tracing pattern.

☐ Using the matting tool depress the shaded blue areas of the design. The matting tool used on this folder gives the stippled texture to the leather.

☐ Smooth over any irregularities with the modeling tool and leave the pieces to dry.

Dyeing. The folder is now dyed using leather dyes (see Leather chapter 9, page 2118).

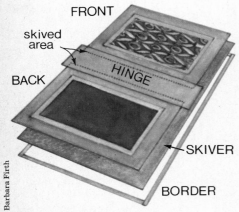

3. *The assembly of the folder.*

Assembling. The pieces are now ready to be glued and stitched together (fig.3).

☐ Glue beveled area of the hinge to back and front before stitching, leaving an extra 2cm ($\frac{3}{4}$") of hinge at each end.

☐ Close the folder and check to see that the edges of the back and front align.

☐ Apply cement to the extra 2cm ($\frac{3}{4}$")

of hinge at each end, fold to the inside and leave to dry.

☐ Following fig.4 scribe stitching lines

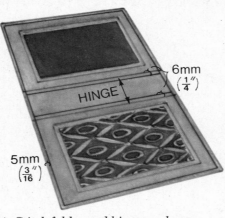

4. *Stitch folder and hinge as shown.*

along the hinge and make stitch marks along the lines using the thonging chisel.

☐ Secure in stitching clams or vise and stitch along the lines using two needles, a stitching awl and waxed thread.

☐ Apply a layer of glue to the inside edges of the folder and to an area the same size on a piece of skiver.

☐ Press the two glued surfaces together.

☐ Trim the skiver to size.

☐ Take the four border strips already cut out and skive down 1cm ($\frac{3}{8}$") at each end of the strips—the longer strips on the flesh side and the shorter strips on the grain side.

☐ Dye the strips to the color of the folder.

☐ Apply glue to a 1cm ($\frac{3}{8}$") border around the inside edge of the folder and to the skin side of the strips.

☐ Place the shorter strips in position first and then the longer ones and allow to dry.

☐ Stitch the strips onto the folder along a line 6mm ($\frac{1}{4}$") from the outside edges. Make the stitching line and marks on the outside of the folder so this will be the neater side (see fig.4).

☐ Apply a coat of wax polish.

The blotter

The blotter measures 60cm x 48cm (24"x 19") and is decorated to match the folder. It will take an average sized piece of blotting paper.

You will need:
Tools as for the folder.
Materials
5mm ($\frac{3}{16}$") thick vegetable-tanned russet cow-hide 60cm x 64cm (24"x 25$\frac{1}{4}$").
Contact cement.
Dyes.
Thread.
Wax and polish as for the folder.

☐ Cut a base piece 60cm x 48cm (24" x 19"), four right-angled triangles (see dotted lines on tracing pattern), and

four strips 1cm ($\frac{3}{8}$") wide, two 21cm (8$\frac{1}{4}$") long and two 33.5cm (13$\frac{1}{4}$") long.

☐ Using the tracing pattern, decorate the pieces for the four corners of the blotter. Make two the same as the pattern and two in mirror image. The two identical triangles will go in diagonally opposite corners.

☐ Dye the triangles, border strips and base piece to match the folder.

☐ Skive the flesh side of both acute-angled corners of each triangle and the grain side of the ends of each strip so that the triangles will fit over the strips (fig.5).

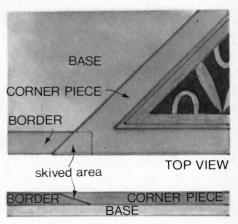

5. *Border pieces slot under corners.*

☐ Apply glue to a 1cm ($\frac{3}{8}$") wide border around the grain side edge of the base piece and to the skin side of the strips. Glue the strips in position (fig.6).

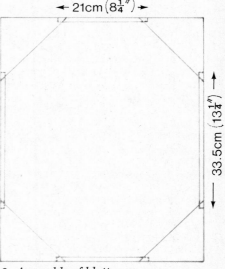

6. *Assembly of blotter.*

☐ Apply glue to a 1cm ($\frac{3}{8}$") border on the flesh side of the triangles on the two shorter sides, and glue in position.

☐ Stitch all around the edge of the blotter along a line 6mm ($\frac{1}{4}$") from the edge.

☐ Apply a coat of wax polish.

Tracing pattern for the folder and blotter corner pieces (marked with the dotted black line).

or smudge. Therefore turn the ruler upside down so that the beveled edge is face down, and hold the pen at right angles to the paper against the edge of the ruler (fig.1).

Left to right: a roll-rule, a pair of rulers hinged together, a transparent plastic ruler and a steel ruler.

Unless straight lines are drawn accurately, the whole proportion and measurements of a design will be incorrect.

A single straight line from one point to another can be drawn using an ordinary steel, plastic or wooden ruler. The edge of the ruler should be placed very slightly below the points to be joined—less than 1mm ($\frac{1}{16}$") away—so that the line drawn against the ruler will actually join the two points.

Parallel lines can be drawn using the method described in Design know-how chapter 6, page 168, or using a special type of ruler.

A roll-role is a ruler attached to **a** cylinder which enables the ruler to **be** rolled up and down the page to draw parallel lines any distance apart. There is a gauge on the cylinder which tells you how far you have moved the ruler.

To draw parallel lines 2.5cm (1") apart, draw the first line and then carefully roll the ruler down the page until the gauge on the cylinder has moved by 2.5cm (1"). At this point, draw the second line which will be parallel to and 2.5cm (1") away from the first line. There is a series of holes 1cm ($\frac{3}{8}$") apart along the edge of the roll-rule. To draw parallel lines 1cm ($\frac{3}{8}$") apart, put the point of a pencil through one of these holes and roll the ruler up or down the page, then put the point of the pencil through the next hole and do the same. It is also possible to buy transparent plastic rulers which have a series of black lines along the length of the ruler, parallel to the edge of the ruler. To draw a pair of parallel lines using this ruler, draw one line, and then place the ruler over the line, so that one of the black lines on the ruler is lying exactly over the drawn line. Draw another line along the edge of the ruler which will be parallel with the first line.

A T-square is another aid to drawing straight and parallel lines. This is a long, flat piece of wood with another piece attached at the other end to make a T shape. The shorter piece of wood can be hooked over the edge of a table or drawing board and slid up and down to draw parallel lines any distance apart.

It is also possible to buy two rulers hinged together so that they can be moved closer together or farther apart while remaining parallel. To use this type of ruler, decide how far apart you want the parallel lines, set the two rulers to this measurement and draw along each edge.

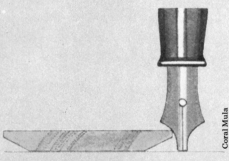

Coral Mula

1. *When drawing a line with a pen, turn the ruler up-side-down.*

Drawing the line. Even when using a ruler it is possible to draw crooked lines by holding your pen or pencil incorrectly. Make sure that the tip of your pencil is at right angles to the paper. When using a pen, however, this method may cause the ink to blot

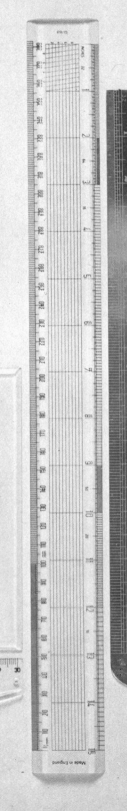

Melvin Grey

Creative ideas 79

Jigsaw puzzles

Use a child's painting on fine cardboard, or an old birthday card for the picture on a jigsaw puzzle.

Before cutting out the shapes, consider whether the puzzle is going to be for a child or an adult and design it to be suitably perplexing.

Keep the finished puzzle in a gift box. Then, if you have two identical pictures, you could paste the second on the box lid.

You will need:
Picture on cardboard.
6mm (¼") plywood, cut to size of picture.
Adhesive such as non-stringing clear mucilage.
Scroll saw.
Fine grade sandpaper.
Clamp or vise, pencil.

Apply adhesive and stick picture to plywood. Leave to dry thoroughly.

In pencil, mark faint guidelines for the puzzle shapes. Secure plywood carefully in clamp or vise. Using a scroll saw cut along guidelines, making sure to use a straight up-and-down movement—so as not to drag against the cardboard.

Smooth down any rough edges on sides and underside of plywood with sandpaper.

If desired, stick an identical picture onto box lid.

Jigsaw puzzles designed by Patricia de Menezes.

Log cabin patchwork

Cloth — patchwork 8

The traditional American method of piecing squares and setting them together to make a quilt is given in Patchwork chapter 7, page 2110. Directions are given in this chapter for a variation on this approach, known as Log Cabin patchwork.

Log Cabin blocks have been set together to form the overall pattern traditionally known as Barn Raising.

Log Cabin follows the block method of quilt construction in so far as square units are built up and then set together. The blocks involved differ from pieced blocks, however, in that they are formed by sewing strips of fabric onto a foundation fabric. The result is known as a 'pressed' block.

Log Cabin, while not the only pressed block, is probably the most common. It is likely that Log Cabin was one of the earliest forms of patchwork, and it was tremendously popular in both America and England during the second half of the 19th century.

A Log Cabin block is made by building up strips of fabric from a central square, their edges overlapping. Traditionally, dark strips are used in one corner, and light strips in the opposite corner, so that the resulting square is divided diagonally into light and dark halves. The central square is thought to represent the fire, the light half the firelit side of the room, and the dark half the shadow.

Suitable fabrics. Victorian Log Cabin quilts were often made with strips of silk and satin ribbons. In fact, this method is sometimes referred to as ribbon patchwork. Cottons, velvet and lightweight wools may also be used, however, and the major advantage of using a foundation fabric which bears the strain is that a mixture of fabrics is also possible.

Quilts made in this way—with each block 'pressed' onto a foundation square—are extremely warm and the strengthening quality of the backing also means that they will stand a reasonable amount of wear.

A Log Cabin block

It is a good idea to practice a few blocks before embarking on a quilt. This will give you confidence in working straight seams, and will help you work out a plan for your quilt. Also, once you have established how much of each fabric is needed for one block, you will be able to estimate your total fabric requirements.

Before making a Log Cabin block, you must first decide on the size of block most suitable for the intended article. Anything from a 15cm (6″) square to a 30cm (12″) square is possible for a quilt. For smaller items such as cushions or trimmings for clothes, a 15cm (6″) square is more appropriate. Having decided on the size of block, you can then proceed to cut out your foundation square and to calculate the required number of fabric strips. These are usually 2.5cm (1″) wide whatever the size of the block.

Accuracy is of the utmost importance in Log Cabin patchwork if you are to obtain true squares which will fit together exactly when joined.

Although it is possible to dispense with templates and simply to measure out the strips of material, it is much safer to make window templates (see Patchwork chapter 3, page 208), allowing a seam allowance all around of 6mm (¼″). Only in this way can you be sure all the strips are exact and match perfectly.

By marking the seam line on the reverse side of the fabric, you will facilitate accurate seaming. Ultimately, window templates are also time saving, since once measured and cut out, they can simply be used again and again for each block, and no further measuring is necessary.

Using fine cotton fabric as a backing fabric, cut out a foundation square of the desired block size, plus 6mm (¼″) seam allowance for joining blocks together at a later stage.

You will need a square of brightly colored fabric for the central square or 'fire'. This is usually twice the width of the strips—5cm (2″) square plus 6mm (¼″) seam allowance all around.

The other fabrics should be cut into strips of 2.5cm (1″) wide plus seam allowance. For each square within the block, you will need two dark strips and two light strips. For each journey around the block, they should be 5cm (2″) longer than the previous four strips.

Thus, if you start with a 5cm (2″) central square (plus seam allowance), you will need four 10cm (4″) long strips (two light, two dark) for the first square, then four 15cm (6″) long strips (two light, two dark) for the next square, and so on—always adding a 6mm (¼″) seam allowance all around—until you have enough strips to fill the foundation square.

To place the strips in the correct position, it is helpful if diagonal pencil or basting lines are made on the foundation fabric from corner to corner, crossing in the center of the square. These lines will act as guides for correct assembly.

Tack the central square accurately to the center of the square of foundation fabric (fig.1).

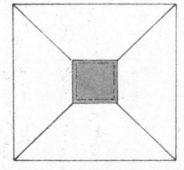

1. *Center square tacked to foundation.*

The first short strip of light fabric should then be placed right side down on the central square, one long edge against one edge of the central square. Pin in position and machine stitch 6mm (¼″) from the edge along the seam line (fig.2).

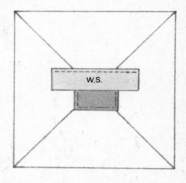

2. *First strip stitched in position.*

It is possible, as with the pieced blocks, to sew the strips by hand in back stitch. The straight seams involved lend themselves particularly well to machine stitching, however, and work obviously progresses more rapidly when a machine is used.

Fold back the first strip and press flat. The second strip of light fabric is sewn along the second side of the central square, overlapping the first strip at the end (fig.3). Fold back and press.

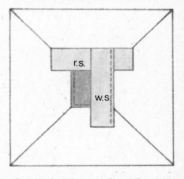

3. *Second strip overlaps first strip.*

Similarly, the third strip—this time of dark fabric—is stitched into position, overlapping the second at one end (fig.4). Fold back and press.

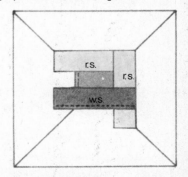

4. *Third strip overlaps second strip.*

The fourth side of the central square is then covered with the fourth strip—of dark fabric again—this time overlapping both the first and third strips at the ends (fig.5). Fold back and press.

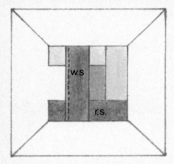

5. Fourth strip completes square.

The process is repeated on the next round, starting on the same side, this time covering the edges of the first row of strips.
Continue covering the foundation square in this way, using two strips of light and two of dark fabric for each square and always starting on the same side of the square. In this way, you will end up with a completely symmetrical pattern, with all the light strips on the opposite diagonal of the completed square (fig.6).

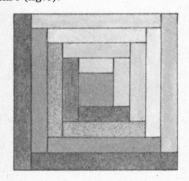

6. Completed Log Cabin block.

The edge of the final strips should meet with the edges of the foundation square. This will, of course, be hidden when the blocks are eventually joined. To ensure a flat finish when joining the blocks later, baste around the edge of the completed block to hold the final strips and the foundation together. Although this arrangement of colors is traditional, there is no reason why you cannot experiment.

Assembling
Log Cabin blocks are always joined or assembled adjacent to each other and are not separated by plain squares or lattice strips as are some of the pieced or appliquéd blocks.
The final design of the quilt is created by the arrangement of the square units, and by the resulting relationship of light and dark shades.

Variations on Log Cabin
Courthouse Steps
The simplest variation on the Log Cabin theme is Courthouse Steps, also known as Washington Steps (fig.7). Here light and dark strips are alternated so that light and dark shades fall on directly opposite sides of the block. The strips of fabric are built up in much the same way as described for Log Cabin.
The overlap of strips is slightly different, however, and necessitates the sewing of strips in opposite pairs, rather than working around the block as for Log Cabin.

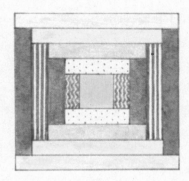

7. A Courthouse Steps block.

'V' pattern
A more unusual design, which only appears to have been popular in Britain, is the 'V' pattern. This is made up by sewing strips in a chevron arrangement.
Light and dark fabrics are stitched alternately in diagonal strips to narrow lengths of foundation material as shown in fig.8a.
The pattern is made by joining the covered lengths so that the strips match in color on each side of the seam to make a V (fig.8b).

a

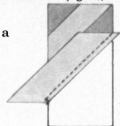

b

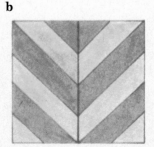

8. Building up the 'V' pattern.

Pineapple
A much more complicated variation is Pineapple, sometimes also known as Windmill Blades (fig.9). The Pineapple block owed its popularity in America to the fact that the pineapple was a traditional symbol of hospitality and was often carved on gate-posts and furniture. The Pineapple quilt was reserved for a guest room, as a sign of welcome.
This block is based on the same principle as Log Cabin in that strips are sewn onto a foundation block of fabric. In this case, however, this is usually bigger—about 45cm (18″) square. It would be difficult to attempt such intricacy within a smaller block.

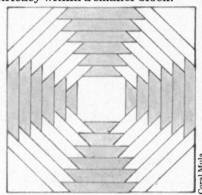

Coral Mula

9. Arrangement of Pineapple block.

The strips are sewn in much the same way as for Log Cabin, but in alternate rows of light and dark colors. This design is particularly effective when worked in one plain color and white. The positioning of strips is slightly different to that of Log Cabin in that on every other journey around the block the strips are laid diagonally across the corners instead of parallel to the sides of the square.
When complete, each square consists of four half 'pineapples'. The whole pineapple pattern only emerges when the blocks are joined.

Finishing
Whatever the design chosen, Log Cabin quilts and variations thereupon often run to the edge of the quilt, without any border.
Because of the presence of a foundation material, the top layer will be very thick. This makes quilting almost impossible.
The quilt should be lined and interlined in the usual way, and then tied instead of quilted (see Patchwork chapter 2, page 182). The positioning of knots should be dictated to a large extent by the design of the quilt, since the knots themselves become an integral part of the pattern
The edges can then be bound in a color echoing one of the colors in the quilt.

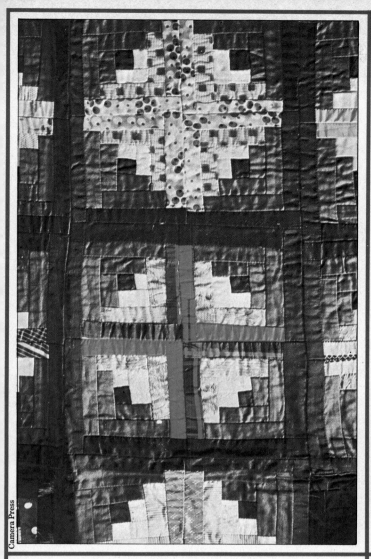

Two similar methods (above and below) of assembling Log Cabin blocks, which result in different overall effects.

Above: traditional Log Cabin set known as Straight Furrow. Below: four Pineapple blocks, designed by Helen Tynan.

Restoring and painting tinware

During the first half of the 18th century the term japanning was used to describe varnishing and art ornamentation on wooden and metal surfaces. Many expensive cabinets and ornate pieces of furniture were imported from the Orient by wealthy Europeans. These were heavily painted with a crimson or black japan, a hard bright lacquer prepared from the sap of an indigenous plant of the sumac species.

Steve Bicknell

The surface of japanned ware was normally decorated with a landscape incorporating waterfalls, houses, trees and plants or simply a gold border or design.

The japan finish was first developed by the Chinese in the 12th century BC. It was not until the 16th century AD that the Japanese far surpassed the original technique and were producing fine quality, lacquered furniture. By the 17th century these items were being imported to Europe and there was suddenly a craze among the ladies of that era for amateur japanning, decorating furniture in the oriental lacquered style.

At the same time in Pontypool in Wales the Allgood family were trying to perfect the japanning technique on tinware. The varnishes and lacquers used on wood would crack and peel off when applied to tin. Finally the breakthrough was made using oxidized linseed oil varnishes hardened by heat treatment, producing a fine hardwearing lacquered finish.

Candlesticks, snuff-boxes, chestnut urns, teapots and coffeepots all emanated from the Allgood workshops in Pontypool and later Usk. But most common of all was the decorated tin tray, which can be easily emulated today. Trays were decorated with all kinds of designs: floral, animal, landscape and coat-of-arms.

It was possible to buy books which had patterns of suitable designs.

In England painted tinware became generally known as Pontypool, but in France, a similar process for *tôle peinte* (painted tinware) was developed by a family named Martin. The name Vernis Martin was applied to all colored lacquering and varnishing, whether on furniture, carriages, snuff-boxes and ultimately on elegant tinware. The Pennsylvania Dutch were noted for their unique designs on tinware in America.

Tôle peinte was hardly seen until the 1790s but then a tremendous variety was prepared—candlesticks, coasters, trays, tea-sets, egg boilers, ewers, basins and cruet stands. Green lacquer with gilding was popular, so too was black with raised gold scrollwork, crimson, blue, blue with gray, yellow and cream. The scenes painted on the *tôle peinte* were very intricate and detailed. Items were often decorated with portraits of the owner.

Japanning tinware on a commercial scale died out at the end of the 19th century. Today using modern lacquers and enamel paints the craft is having a small-scale revival.

Decorating tinware

Tin trays are cheap to buy and can be fun to decorate. Another idea is to decorate tin cans.

You will need:
Tinware to be decorated.
Red oxide paint.
Wet or Dry paper, fine.
Professional painter's drop cloth (similar to a fine cheesecloth).

A feature of antique trays is their deep, rich sheen. This was achieved by polishing the lacquered surface with natural resins and oils.

Enamel paint for background (or japan oil paints).
A good quality, fine, outlining brush.
Gold paint such as liquid gold leaf.
Gold sealer.
A selection of artist's oil paints including black oil-based enamel and burnt umber.
Wax furniture polish.
Tracing paper.
Hard pencil and soft pencil.
Powdered chalk.
Eggshell varnish.

Preparation. To prepare raw tinware, apply a coat of the rust inhibitor red oxide paint to the entire object. Leave to dry.

☐ When it is dry sand it lightly with Wet or Dry paper.

☐ Apply a second coat of red oxide paint, and again when dry sand it lightly with Wet or Dry paper.

☐ Remove all dust particles with a professional painter's cloth.

☐ Next apply the background of enamel paint (the color used should depend on the decoration design you have selected).

☐ Sand the first coat after you have left it to dry for at least 24 hours. Dust with a soft cloth.

☐ Apply two more coats of enamel.

☐ When the final coat is dry rub the surface down with Wet or Dry paper to remove the gloss.

Select a design. Place the tracing paper over the design and trace it using a hard pencil so that the lines are clear.

☐ Turn over the tracing paper and rub with powdered chalk if you are using a dark background or soft lead pencil if you are using a light background.

☐ Tape the tracing of the design, chalk or lead side down, to the object.

☐ Using a hard pencil, go over the design very carefully so that it is transferred clearly onto the article).

☐ Using the artist's oil paints, paint your design. Use firm definite strokes. It is worthwhile practicing on a scrap of paper before attempting the design on the tinware.

☐ The gold lines should be added once the main design is complete. Whether it is elaborate or simple it should be applied with a firm, definite stroke so you do not end up with hesitant, wobbly lines. To aid drawing straight lines use artist's masking tape, leaving the area of the line unmasked.

☐ When the gold has dried seal it with gold sealer otherwise it will soften and be shifted by the varnish.

Varnish. Apply a coat of eggshell varnish, tinted with a little black and burnt umber oil paint.

When the varnish is dry, polish the surface with a wax polish. This will give a much pleasanter effect than a gloss varnish.

Tin kitchen utensils are fun and cheap to decorate.

Decorated domestic tinware brightens up a kitchen.

Restoring tinware

It is quite possible to find interesting pieces of tinware in antique and junk shops. Often they will be dented, rusty and rather battered and will therefore be inexpensive. However they may well be Victorian-style ware or perhaps even *tôle peinte*.

The most likely items you will find are trays and candle holders but boxes, letter racks, urns and teapots are quite common. Some of the finest pieces made in the last century are coal-scuttles which were an important part of Victorian life, and were often over-decorated like so much Victoriana.

All these items are worth restoring but it is no simple matter to restore or recreate this type of decoration since the original decoration was applied by stencil or tracing and requires a steady hand and sure touch to achieve the precise effect.

The preparation of all tinware is basically the same providing the piece is sound.

It is important to start with a smooth base as you will want to finish with the glossiest, most lacquered effect possible.

You will need:

Paint stripper or medium grit Carborundum® paper.

Fine surface commercial cellulose plaster filler.

Wet or Dry paper (fine).

Enamel paint for background (or oil-based japan paints).

Soft cloth.

Quite often on a piece of tinware a crude attempt has been made to overpaint the decoration where it has been scratched or damaged.

☐ Carefully remove all traces of paint with paint stripper or medium grit carborundum or garnet paper until the tin is exposed.

☐ Scratches and dents should be filled in with plaster filler; do not attempt to hammer them out.

☐ Rub down the entire surface with Wet or Dry paper until it is smooth and even.

☐ Remove any dust or grit with a soft cloth.

☐ When the base is smooth and clean, apply the first coat of enamel paint. It is wisest to stick to the traditional japan colors, black, crimson, green or a very dark blue. Whatever background you use it must be a color which will show off gold to advantage.

☐ Once the first coat of paint is dry, rub it down lightly with Wet or Dry paper to remove any specks.

☐ Apply two more coats of enamel

paint, allow the first to dry before applying the second.

It is sometimes easier to use an aerosol paint for a smooth finish.

☐ When the final coat of enamel is dry rub it down very lightly with Wet or Dry paper to remove the gloss.

Decoration. Try to stick as close to the original style of decoration as possible. If the piece has been overpainted it is worth attempting to remove the paint carefully to find out if the original decoration has survived sufficiently to guide your restoration.

On a piece which is intrinsically attractive it is advisable to stick to a clear and unfussy style of decoration and to avoid the use of too much color.

If you are not copying your design from an actual piece (freehand or tracing), it is well worth taking the time and trouble to work it out on paper before commencing your decorating.

The basic method of decoration will be the same as that for modern tinware. Paint on your design with great delicacy to avoid a crude appearance. The gold lining can be quite simple or can consist of elaborate borders like the examples on the coal-scuttle and the small tray.

It can be highlighted with minute spots of white on the joins and crossings and pink or white spots in the center of the flowers.

Domestic tinware

While searching for antique decorative tinware, you are quite likely to come across some basic domestic tinware that has been japanned. Foot baths, water cans, hip baths and cream pans are all good examples of japanned domestic tinware worth restoring and decorating.

Preparation. The preparation for these cruder pieces should be more thorough than for display ware as they have usually had a rougher life and were often used to contain water. They are liable to be rusty, usually around the seams.

You will need:

A rust remover.
Medium grit Carborundum® or garnet paper.
Wet or Dry paper (fine).
Red oxide paint.
Car body filler (plastic padding).
Enamel paint for the background.

☐ Following the manufacturer's instructions use the commercial rust remover first.
☐ Rub the entire surface with medium grit Carborundum® paper.
☐ Apply a coat of red oxide paint.
☐ Fill holes and dents with car body filler (carefully follow the instructions).
☐ With the medium grit carborundum paper rub down the surface until it is smooth and level.
☐ Apply three coats of the background color.
☐ Rub down with Wet or Dry paper to prepare for decoration.

Decoration. Traditionally most domestic tinware was finished with a wood grain effect. But this does not necessarily mean it has to be restored to this state, unless you wish it to be authentic. An exception to this is the foot bath which is usually decorated with flowers in the manner of its porcelain cousin. These are quite finely painted. If you are unable to obtain this effect with flowers it might be better to stick to a formal pattern or simply a border.

Tin water pitchers make charming watering cans for indoor plants and are best decorated with a simple classical border.

Hip baths can be decorated with fish or shells and the outside can be painted and lined in different colors.

The styles of decorating tinware range from the simple, colorful folk technique used for kitchen utensils and drinking vessels, to the more sophisticated japanning found on decorative display ware. Bear in mind the origins and traditional color schemes used before planning any decoration.

Once restored, hip baths and cream pans make attractive and original containers.

The elaborate gold borders on this coal-scuttle were applied using a stencil.

Steve Bicknell

2221

Colorful modern smocking

Smocking is a method of decorating a band of fabric which has been gathered into a series of tiny pleats. It derives from the loose linen smocks once worn by country workmen. These smocks were made from wide panels of fabric which were gathered into a yoke.

To offset their plainness the gathers were decorated with simple embroidery. The embroidery also held the gathers in place so the original gathering threads could be removed, allowing for more ease in the smocked band. Extra decorative stitchery was worked on the yoke and sleeves of the smock, often in motifs denoting the trade of the wearer. (Instructions for making a traditional smock are given in a later chapter.)

Today smocking is often worked to decorate gathered fullness on babies' and children's clothes and at the necks and yokes of blouses and the cuffs and heads of sleeves.

It can also be worked on the ruffle of a bedspread or for a curtain border.

Unlike traditional smocking which was nearly always worked on white or natural-colored fabrics with matching embroidery, modern smocking can be colorful worked on printed fabrics and the embroidery in matching colors.

The smocking is always worked before the garment is made up.

Materials

Fabrics. Smocking can be worked on any fabric which can be gathered easily, such as voile, lawn, linen, silk and fine woolen fabrics.

Smocking can also be worked on heavy fabrics such as velvet, corduroy or even suede or leather if you are prepared to experiment on a spare piece to find the best method for gathering and suitable smocking stitches.

Amount of fabric. Generally, three times the required finished width should be allowed but this may vary according to the kind of fabric and the stitches being used. (If you are adapting a pattern in order to include a smocked section, measure the section to which it will be attached and allow three times this width.)

On heavy fabrics, however, where the gathering stitches are spaced farther apart, the fullness may be reduced to two or two-and-a-half times the required finished width.

Threads. Use a soft embroidery thread or pearl cotton for the embroidery and a strong sewing cotton for the gathering stitches. Stranded embroidery thread is less suitable for the embroidery.

Preparing the fabric

The fabric must be carefully gathered into pleats to ensure a neat finish to the smocking. The pleats are formed by several rows of evenly spaced gathering stitches. The working of these gathering stitches may be based on the weave of the fabric, either by counting threads or—on close checked, striped on polka dot fabrics—by using the pattern as a guide.

Alternatively a grid of dots showing the positions of the gathering stitches should be marked on the fabric. This can be done either by hand-marking them with a pencil and ruler or by ironing on a commercially printed guide-dot transfer. Either method is satisfactory providing the rows of dots lie exactly on the straight grain of the fabric.

Spacing the stitches. For most fabrics the stitches should be about 5mm ($\frac{3}{16}''$) apart although closely spaced stitches —about 3mm ($\frac{1}{8}''$) apart—should be used for fine fabrics such as voile and lawn. More widely spaced stitches— up to 22mm ($\frac{7}{8}''$) apart—should be used on thicker fabrics.

The spacing between the rows of stitches is a matter of preference and, providing that the fabric is pleated correctly, it does not matter if the rows are quite widely spaced—up to 2cm ($\frac{3}{4}''$) apart. Closer rows, however, are often helpful because they act as a guide to stitching the embroidery.

Always work a row of gathering along the top and bottom edges of the smocking.

Commercial transfers are made with the guide-dots and rows in a variety of spacings to suit different fabrics.

The gathering

All gathering is done on the wrong side of the fabric, in horizontal rows and working from right to left (if you are right handed). Use a strong thread and knot the end securely before beginning each row. At the end of each row cut off the thread leaving about 5cm (2") hanging loose.

Counting threads. Use this method on coarse or loosely woven fabrics where you can see the threads easily.

☐ Make a tiny stitch of two or three threads, pass the needle along the fabric counting the threads to leave the desired space and make another small stitch of the same size as the first.

☐ Continue like this to the end of the row, always counting threads so that stitches and spaces are of constant sizes.

☐ Work subsequent rows in the same way so that all stitches lie directly in line with those in the rows above.

Checked fabrics. Use this method on checks up to 12mm ($\frac{1}{2}''$) square.

☐ If you wish the darkest colour of the fabric to be prominent in the finished smocking, place the gathering stitches in the centre of the palest squares.

☐ If you wish the darkest color of the fabric to be prominent in the finished smocking, place the gathering stitches in the center of the palest squares.

☐ If you prefer a pale background, place the stitches in the middle of the darkest squares.

Stripes. Use the same method on stripes up to 12mm ($\frac{1}{2}''$) wide and follow the principle as for checked fabrics.

Polka dots. Suitable for use on fabrics where polka dots are small and woven in close rows up to 12mm ($\frac{1}{2}''$) apart. Work the rows of gathering on alternate rows of dots so that the stitches in each row will be in line with each other. Work the stitches from one dot to the next in each row.

Marked dots. Work as for polka dots but with a row of gathering to each row of dots. Make a tiny stitch at each dot before passing onto the next dot (fig.1).

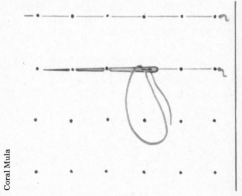

Coral Mula

1. *Working the gathering stitches.*

These two adorable little girls' dresses are made in a gingham and a patterned cotton, with smocking designs by Cheryl Fry.

Drawing up the gathers. When all the rows of gathering have been worked, pull up all the threads (fig.2) until the fabric is slightly narrower than the desired width (it will slacken slightly with the embroidery).

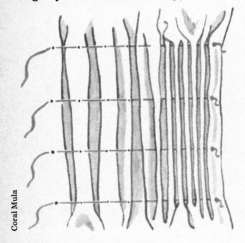

Coral Mula

2. Drawing up the gathering threads.

☐ Insert a pin at the end of each row and wind the ends of threads in a figure eight around them. If the pleats are not tightly packed even them out across the width.

☐ Turn the fabric to the right side for working the embroidery.

Embroidery stitches

There are several stitches which may be used for decorating the gathering. Most of them are variations of stem stitch and are sometimes known by the type of pattern they form (see box).

Each stitch holds or controls the gathers by a different amount or tension. A firm-control stitch, for example, secures the gathers firmly and there is little give.

Most smocking designs use a mixture of stitches and it is advisable to place a firm-control stitch along the top and bottom of the area. One exception to this might be around the neck of a baby's dress where you wish the smocked area to be flared. In this case a firm-control stitch should be used along the top and a loose-control stitch along the bottom.

Note: where the stitch instructions specify a direction for working the row or for inserting the needle, these should be reversed for left-handed workers.

Finishing smocking

When all the decorative stitches have been worked, place the fabric right side down on a thick blanket. Lay a damp cloth over it and press very lightly with a hot iron to set the pleats. Pull out the gathering stitches.

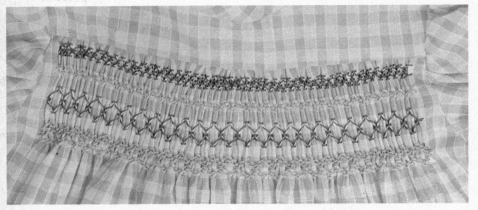

Smocking worked in surface honeycomb (top), feather and diamond stitches.

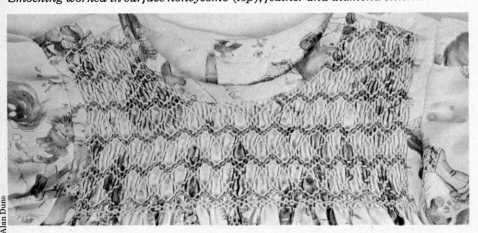

Alan Duns

Smocking worked in diamond pattern and double cable stitches (bottom).

Outline or rope stitch

This is a firm-control stitch, often used for the top and bottom lines of a smocked design to hold the pleats in place.

☐ Following fig.3a and working from left to right, bring the needle through to the right side of the fabric on the left-hand side of pleat 1 as indicated.

☐ With the thread above the needle, insert through pleat 2 from right to left. Pull up slightly.

☐ Continue in this way, taking one pleat at a time (fig.3b).

Cable and basket stitch

This is a firm-control stitch also suitable for the top and bottom lines of a smocking design.

☐ Following fig.4a and working from left to right, bring the needle through on the left-hand side of pleat 1. Keeping the thread above the needle, insert the needle through pleat 2 from right to left. Pull up the thread.

☐ Keeping the thread below the needle, insert the needle through pleat 3 from right to left.

☐ Continue in this way, inserting the needle through each pleat with the thread above and below alternately. Pull up the thread after each stitch to form a smooth line (fig.4b).

Double cable stitch

This is made by two rows of cable stitch worked close together. Start the second row with the thread *below* the needle and continue alternately as before (fig.5).

Diamond pattern

This is a loose-control stitch formed by combining outline stitches in a wave pattern and cable stitches to create diamonds in the design.

☐ Insert the needle through the pleats from right to left. When working downward, keep the thread above the needle (fig.6). When working upward, insert the needle with the thread below it.

Honeycomb stitch

This is an elastic stitch and is one of the best known smocking stitches. The stitches are worked alternately between two rows of gathering.

☐ Working from left to right, bring the needle through to the right side of the fabric through pleat 1. Keeping the thread above the needle, insert the needle through pleats 2 and 1 from right to left (fig.7a) and pull up together.

☐ Insert the needle through pleat 2 again on the right-hand side and pass the thread to come out through pleat 2 on the second row of gathering.

☐ With the thread below the needle,

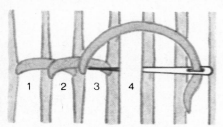

3a. *Starting outline stitch.*

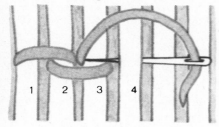

4a. *Starting cable stitch.*

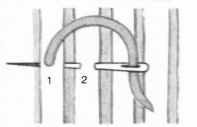

5. *Double cable stitch.*

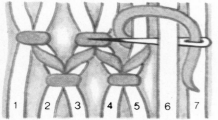

7a. *Starting honeycomb stitch.*

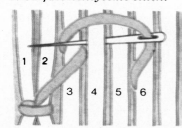

9b. *Continuing diamond stitch.*

stitch pleats 3 and 2 as for pleats 2 and 1 in the row above. Pass the needle on the wrong side to come out through pleat 3 on the first row

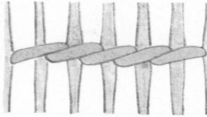

3b. *Outline stitch finished.*

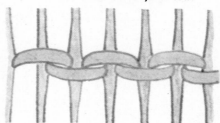

4b. *Cable stitch finished.*

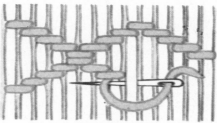

6. *Diamond pattern.*

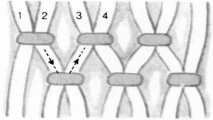

7b. *Honeycomb stitch finished.*

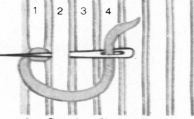

9a. *Starting diamond stitch.*

10. *Double diamond stitch.*

of gathering.

☐ Continue in this way taking two pleats together on each stitch and alternating between each row of gathering (fig.7b).

Surface honeycomb stitch

This is similar to ordinary honeycomb stitch except that the thread connecting the stitches is worked on the right side of the fabric so only one stitch need be worked over the pleats (fig.8).

☐ Working from left to right, bring the needle to the right side of the fabric to the left of pleat 1. With the thread above the needle make a back stitch on pleat 2 and pull the pleats together.

☐ Take the thread to pleat 2 on the second row and insert it from right to left. Keeping the thread below the needle, insert through pleat 3 from right to left. Pull the pleats together.

☐ Return to the first row and insert the needle through pleat 3. With the thread above the needle, work through pleat 4 as before.

☐ Continue working alternately between the rows in this way.

Feather stitch

Work as shown in Embroidery chapter 6, page 802, for a fairly tight smocking stitch.

☐ Work from left to right, picking up two pleats of fabric in each stitch. For double feather stitch work two stitches to each side alternately.

Diamond stitch

This is a loose-control stitch worked on two rows of gathering. Working from left to right, bring through the needle on the left-hand side of pleat 1 on the second row of gathering. Work one back stitch on this pleat with the thread above the needle and one stitch on pleat 2 with the thread below the needle (fig.9a). Draw the pleats together.

☐ Take the thread to the first row of gathering and insert the needle through pleat 3 from right to left with the thread below the needle and then through pleat 4 with the thread above the needle (fig.9b).

☐ Return to the second row of gathering and work through pleats 5 and 6.

☐ Continue in this way, working between the rows alternately.

Double diamond stitch

This is worked by placing the stitches between those worked first. It looks most attractive when stitched in a contrasting color (fig.10).

Introduction to shellcraft

There are very few people who, after a summer by the sea, have not wanted to take home shells to remind them of their holiday. Shells, as souvenirs, will always remain as beautiful as when they were found, but it is often a problem knowing what to do with them. All too frequently they eventually find their way into the garbage.

However, shell collections can be central to a craft which is becoming more and more popular. There are several reasons for the renewed interest in shellcraft: people are more widely traveled than ever before and have been to beaches abroad; also shells are being exported from their native habitats to other countries (the Philippines exports the greatest number of shells). Recently many stores have been opened which specialize in selling shells as art objects and collector's items.

Shell collecting is an occupation which goes back thousands of years to when shells, especially cowries, were used as a medium of exchange. The North American Indian used to use shell beads called 'wampum' for currency. In many parts of the world, shells have also been used as cooking pots, drinking vessels, dishes, musical instruments, jewelry and as sacred objects.

Shells have always been symbols of love (Venus is said to have been born in a shell off the island of Cyprus) and of good luck.

Shells can be used to decorate many household objects such as boxes, vases and other items, and to make collages, pictures, figurines and jewelry. Decorative uses for different types of shell are fully discussed in several later chapters.

The mollusks

Shells are to be found on the land as well as in fresh water and the sea. They come in many colors, shapes and sizes. Zoologically they are classed as *Phylum Mollusca*, or mollusks. The mollusk itself is a soft-bodied animal without a backbone (an invertebrate) which has to compensate for its unprotected state by building a hard shell around itself. This is the external 'skeleton' of the animal.

There are more than 100,000 known species of mollusk, but these can be conveniently divided into six families or classes. Most of the shells found by collectors fall into the first two families listed here.

Gastropods. The gastropods (meaning 'belly-footed') are a group of univalves (meaning 'one shell') whose single shell is usually in a spiral shape. They make up three-quarters of the world's shells. Typical gastropods are snails, species of which are found on land as well as in the sea, and some even in trees. Most gastropods, which include conches, cowries, cones, whelks and top shells, move along on a muscular pad-like foot.

Pelecypods. The pelecypods (meaning 'hatchet-footed') are all bivalves (meaning 'two shells'), and have a pair of hinged shells. They include oysters, mussels, clams and scallops. Because they tend to be sedentary they often grow to considerable size.

Scaphopods. These are also known as tusk shells because their shape resembles the tusk of an elephant. They live only in the sea.

Amphineura. These are the 'coat of mail' shells or chitons. The chiton's shell is made up of overlapping scales, suggesting the idea of a coat of armor. Chitons are usually quite colorful.

Cephalopods. Cephalopods (meaning 'head-footed') are the most highly developed of all molluscs. They include the shell-less octopus, squid, cuttlefish, paper nautilus (argonaut) and the beautiful chambered nautilus. Pearlized pieces known as 'nautilus drops' are cut from the chambered nautilus and it can be split down the middle to reveal the separate chambers which it builds as it grows.

Monoplacophora. This rare deep-sea species was known only as a fossil until recently.

Pseudo shells

Pseudo shells come from animals which have shells but which are not molluscs. The shells are often very decorative and can be used by the collector in many ways. They include starfish, which are found in all oceans. Sea-urchins also have pseudo shells which can be dyed very successfully.

Horseshoe crabs and other common crabs often have very colorful shells which can be used complete, as a decoration, or broken up into small pieces which can be used in a mosaic or picture. Sea-horses, which are

From left to right (top to bottom): cross-section of a chambered nautilus; cowrie; scallop; abalone; mussel; two limpets; murex; cockle; two cowries; conch; murex; chiton; two top shells; helmet shell.

native to the waters off southern Florida and other tropical seas, can be dried and used in jewelry making or embedded in clear plastic to make attractive paper-weights and pendants. Turtles, and to a lesser extent tortoises, are the source of one of the most attractive types of shell, called tortoise-shell. This is often available from shell shops and is sold in small pieces or flakes which usually come from the hawk's-bill turtle. However, you may be able to find a whole shell, called a carapace or 'roof', in an antique shop.

Coral is also available in many different varieties from shell shops. Coral is a limestone marine formation made by animals called polyps.

Choosing shells

Before starting to acquire a collection of shells for craft purposes it is important to think of all shells in relation to five basic qualities. These are structure, color, iridescence (the quality of reflecting light in a pearly sheen possessed by certain shells such as the pearl oyster), size and rarity.

Whether you are more interested in color or shape depends very much on your own taste but it is nevertheless a good idea to have examples of both in your collection.

The size of shells you choose will often depend on what room you have to display them. You will probably have to buy rare shells but they can be quite expensive.

Where to find shells

The most obvious place to look for shells is on a beach, and the species you find will vary according to the region you are in and the locality.

Rocky beaches with cliffs, rock pools and large boulders are more rewarding hunting grounds than sandy beaches. Search in rock pools for living shells rather than on the shore-line. Sea-washed shells will almost certainly have become discolored or chipped, although they may often have holes worn in their tips which make them suitable for threading. It is a good idea to read an illustrated identification handbook for your particular area, so that you know what to look for before

you start.

In American waters the Gulf and Atlantic coasts will yield Florida top shells, Cayenne keyhole limpets, smooth tops, long-spined star shells, bleeding tooths, American star shells, quahogs, zebra periwinkles, worm shells, horns, spotted slippers, white slippers, conches, moon shells, murex shells, paper nautili and many others far too numerous to mention. The quahog is the only shell from which wampum can be made.

The Pacific coast is also an important source of many varieties of shell, the most important of which is the abalone. This is a beautiful iridescent shell from which a great deal of shell jewelry is made.

On British shores look for limpets, periwinkles, cockles, razor shells, tellins, whelks, scallops and winkles. These are shells with a strong structure which can be used in collage, on mirror frames and in bold displays. Other useful British shells are native oysters, purple caps, mussels, saddle oysters, top shells, ormers and otter or gaper shells. All of these are iridescent

Beach-combing on the Mediterranean coast of Morocco. Children will enjoy searching for particular types of shell and may even present you with real 'finds'.

Michael Boys

except gaper shells which have a very thick, white porcelaneous wall. They can be ground into pieces for jewelry or broken into chips for mosaic.

Australian waters provide many shells which are well worth collecting for craft work because of their bright colors or iridescence and beautiful shapes. They include giant clams, cone shells, cowries, turban snails and volutes. The pearl oyster, the most widely used iridescent shell from which most mother of pearl buttons are made, comes from Australia.

South African shores, which face both the Atlantic and the Indian Ocean, have a great many varieties of shell. Turret shells, conches, volutes, murex shells, cowries, cones and Venus shells are a few of the most common.

Equipment. When beach-combing, take a small crow-bar for turning over boulders and hooking under rocky ledges. Pack the shells in small cardboard boxes and tissue paper or cotton so that they will not get chipped or broken.

Carry a knapsack or some other container in which to hold everything.

These shell beads are used as money by the Solomon islanders.

Buying shells

Even if you do not live near the sea you can collect shells by buying them, either direct or by mail order. Many collectors buy shells to add to their collection of shells which they have found. The advantages of buying are that a very wide selection is available from all over the world and that the shells will be already cleaned and polished, ready to display immediately.

Cleaning shells

To prepare shells for any ornamental purposes the animal inside them must first be removed along with the smell of decay. The shell must also be cleaned in order to bring out its true colors, and polished or varnished so that it shines.

There are various ways of cleaning shells:

Tiny shells such as periwinkles are best soaked in a solution of 80 per cent alcohol and 20 per cent water before the animal is pulled out with tweezers.

To clean bivalves, simply place them in fresh water for 30 minutes, then pry them open and scrape out the meat with a knife, before scrubbing them.

Univalves. One of the easiest and quickest ways of cleaning larger univalves is to boil them as soon as possible after returning home from the beach, before removing the animal.

You will need:
A nylon or string mesh bag.
An old saucepan.
Water.
Crochet hook or tweezers or a piece of hooked wire.
Vegetable or nail brush (for larger shells), a toothbrush (for smaller shells).
Liquid detergent.
Chlorine (optional).
Wax polish or clear polyurethane varnish and brush.
Soft rags.

☐ Put shells of similar size in the bag to prevent them moving around in the boiling water and possibly chipping or breaking.

☐ Place the bag and shells in a pan of boiling water. Boil shells less than 10cm (4″) long for no more than five minutes, larger shells for ten to 15 minutes.

☐ When they have finished boiling, remove the shells from the boiling water and hold them (still inside the bag) under cold running water to cool.

☐ With tweezers, crochet hook or hooked wire, gently pull the animal slowly out of its shell. Try to remove the animal in one piece; it is much more difficult to pull out if you break off part of it. You know that the whole animal is out if its tip comes to a point.

To wash the shell use detergent and hot water. Use a toothbrush to brush the smaller shells and a vegetable or nail brush for the larger ones. Make sure that all foreign matter is removed.

☐ In order to bleach shells and remove their periostracum (outside coating), soak them in a strong solution of chlorine for a few hours. However, this will discolor colored shells so use this method only for white shells.

☐ Rinse the shells, dry them thoroughly and polish them with a soft cloth. Wax polish rubbed over a shell will help to bring out its surface pattern and colors. If you prefer, you can apply two coats of clear polyurethane varnish to the shell instead of wax polish.

Grading shells

When collecting shells for display and decoration it is wise to ignore the zoological classifications although it is useful to know them. Classify them according to their potential use, which will be as decorations, jewelry, mosaic, collage or picture elements, figurines or for covering containers.

Handbags from soft leather

Sandra Lousada

Making handbags from soft leather is simple, straightforward and many styles can be made entirely by hand if you do not have a sewing machine. Most leather handbags are made from soft skins—only a very sturdy type of handbag intended for casual wear is made with thick hide.

This chapter tells you how to make the clutch bag (see photograph) which is a classic handbag shape involving basic techniques, such as putting in a gusset and attaching a lining. This basic shape can be adapted to a different size or given zipper, fasteners, handles, or shoulder straps if desired.

The clutch bag

This clutch bag measures 29cm x 16cm (11½″ x 6¼″). Directions are given here for assembling the basic bag shape and inserting a cloth lining. The appliqué design on the bag flap can be attached or left off as desired.

You will need:

Light-weight clothing leather at least 83cm x 30cm (34″x 12″) from which to cut the pattern pieces (fig.1).

Skiver the same size for backing the leather.

Leather for appliqué (fig.2). This can be obtained from bags of scraps which are sold by some leather suppliers (optional).

45cm (½yd) of lining fabric, 1m (36″) wide—buy a fairly heavy lining fabric such as taffeta to withstand wear and tear.

Mercerized cotton thread, in colors to match the leather you are using for the bag and also to match any appliqué leathers.

Sewing machine with size 16 wedge-shaped needle, such as made by Singer® for machine stitching.

Glover's needle and betweens needle for hand stitching.

Thimble.

Cardboard from which to cut pattern pieces, at least 78cm x 30cm (31″ x 12″).

A sharp knife.

Ballpoint pen.

Sharp pencil.

Steel ruler.

Rubber-based glue.

Transparent adhesive tape or paper clips.

Pair of sharp scissors.

Triangle.

Tailor's chalk.

☐ Using a triangle and ruler, draw the pattern shapes (fig.1) onto the cardboard and cut them out. It is essential that each piece should have straight edges and right-angled corners.

The flap of this simple clutch bag is decorated with an attractive appliqué pattern in subtly blending colors. Designed by Lesley Slight.

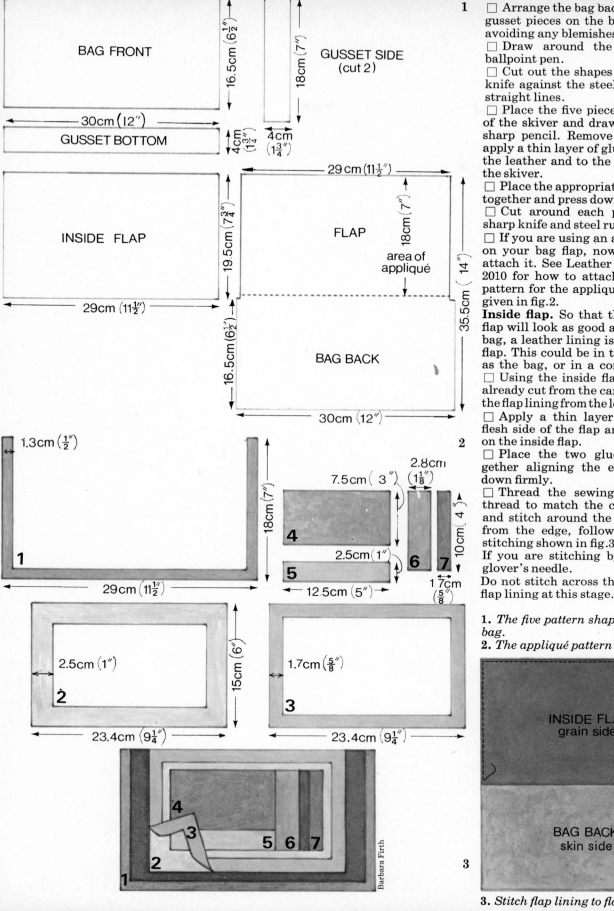

BAG FRONT

16.5cm (6½")

30cm (12")

GUSSET SIDE (cut 2)

18cm (7")

4cm (1¾")

GUSSET BOTTOM

4cm (1¾")

INSIDE FLAP

19.5cm (7¾")

29cm (11½")

29cm (11½")

FLAP

18cm (7")

area of appliqué

35.5cm (14")

16.5cm (6½")

BAG BACK

30cm (12")

1.3cm (½")

1

18cm (7")

29cm (11½")

7.5cm (3")

4

2.8cm (1⅛")

2

2.5cm (1")

15cm (6")

23.4cm (9¼")

2.5cm (1")

5

12.5cm (5")

6

10cm (4")

7

1.7cm (⅝")

1.3cm (½")

3

1.7cm (⅝")

23.4cm (9¼")

4

3

2

1

5 6 7

Barbara Firth

1

☐ Arrange the bag back, bag front and gusset pieces on the back of the skin, avoiding any blemishes or faults.

☐ Draw around the pieces with a ballpoint pen.

☐ Cut out the shapes using the sharp knife against the steel ruler to obtain straight lines.

☐ Place the five pieces onto the back of the skiver and draw around with a sharp pencil. Remove the pieces and apply a thin layer of glue to the back of the leather and to the marked area on the skiver.

☐ Place the appropriate glued surfaces together and press down firmly.

☐ Cut around each piece using the sharp knife and steel ruler.

☐ If you are using an appliqué pattern on your bag flap, now is the time to attach it. See Leather chapter 7, page 2010 for how to attach appliqué. The pattern for the appliqué on this bag is given in fig.2.

Inside flap. So that the inside of the flap will look as good as the rest of the bag, a leather lining is attached to the flap. This could be in the same leather as the bag, or in a contrasting color.

☐ Using the inside flap pattern piece already cut from the cardboard, cut out the flap lining from the leather as before.

☐ Apply a thin layer of glue to the flesh side of the flap and to the skiver on the inside flap.

☐ Place the two glued surfaces together aligning the edges and press down firmly.

☐ Thread the sewing machine with thread to match the color of the bag and stitch around the flap, 1mm (1/16") from the edge, following the line of stitching shown in fig.3.

If you are stitching by hand use the glover's needle.

Do not stitch across the bottom of the flap lining at this stage.

1. *The five pattern shapes for the clutch bag.*

2. *The appliqué pattern shapes.*

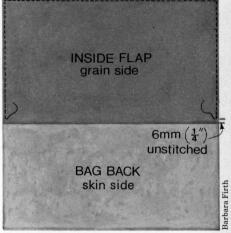

INSIDE FLAP grain side

6mm (¼") unstitched

BAG BACK skin side

Barbara Firth

3

3. *Stitch flap lining to flap.*

□ The other bag pieces are now ready to be stitched together. These pieces are stitched right sides together leaving a seam allowance of 5mm ($\frac{1}{4}''$). See Leather chapter 7, page 2010 for how to stitch soft leather.

□ First of all stitch along the top of the front piece, about 1mm ($\frac{1}{16}''$) from the edge. This line of stitching is done to give the bag a neat 'finished' look.

□ Secure the seams while stitching with paper clips or clear adhesive tape.

□ Stitch the gusset pieces together to make one long strip of leather.

□ Measure the gusset side pieces against the sides of the front piece and draw a line on the wrong side of the gusset piece to mark where it should end. Do the same on the other side.

□ Apply a thin layer of glue to the

The flap on this clutch bag follows the outline of the appliqué flowers and leaves. Designed by Nigel Lofthouse.

wrong side of the ends of the gusset piece, turn over along the drawn line and press down firmly.

□ The gusset can now be stitched to the front piece.

So that the gusset will be central on the front piece, the stitching is done in three stages.

□ Stitch the center gusset piece to the bottom of the front piece making sure that the corners correspond with the seams on the gusset.

□ Then stitch the sides from the bottom corners up to the top (fig.4).

□ Stitch the bag back to the assembled gusset and bag front. In the same way

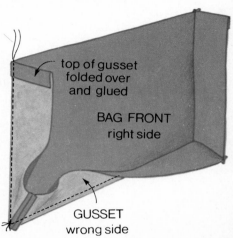

top of gusset folded over and glued

BAG FRONT right side

GUSSET wrong side

4. *Gusset attached to bag front.*

as before stitch the bottom of the bag back to the bottom of the gusset, making sure that the corners of the back piece correspond with the seams on the gusset, and then stitch up each side.

□ Turn the bag the right way around and firmly press out the corners.

The lining

Once the bag is assembled, the lining is attached. Lining can be attached by hand or by machine. It is easier to attach a lining by hand, and this is the method used here.

□ Cut out the lining—two bag front pieces and the three gusset pieces. Cut generously to allow for a slightly larger seam allowance.

□ Mark the seam allowance with

Art deco designs made with stenciling and appliqué of different textures of leather. The bags are by Nigel Lofthouse.

tailor's chalk and stitch the lining together.

□ Draw a line across the inside flap level with the top of the gusset. This leaves a 5mm (¼") seam allowance.

□ Turn the bag lining the right way around and place on top of the inside flap (fig.5).

□ Stitch the lining to the flap lining following the line of stitching marked in fig.5.

□ Push the lining into the bag and turn in the raw edge of the lining so that it is slightly below the bag's top.

□ Slip-stitch the lining to the top of the bag.

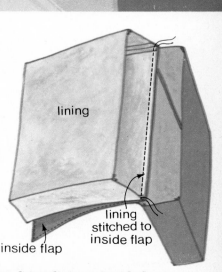

lining

lining stitched to inside flap

inside flap

5. *Stitch lining to inside flap.*

Introducing corn dollies

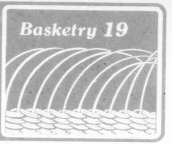

Corn dollies were made as long ago as 5000 years. They are found in various forms all over the world. They were generally made as fertility symbols. After the last sheaf of the harvest was cut it would be made into a corn dolly and great feasting and celebration would take place. Ceres, the goddess of the harvest, was thought to live in the corn dollies which were kept indoors during winter to protect the goddess.

In the spring the corn dollies would be cast into the fields so that the goddess could help germinate the new corn.

Corn dollies were also used as sacrifices or in worship to a pagan god. Examples of corn dollies have been found in Mexico in the form of angels; Germany and Scandinavia also produced decorative objects made from corn and in Bulgaria they were made from maize. Corn dollies are not necessarily made in the form of 'dolls', but in a number of traditional, often symbolic shapes. The word doll or dolly is in fact a corruption of the word 'idol'.

In England, for example, different parts of the country made different types of corn dollies which have become traditional. A lantern is associated with Norfolk county but a variation of it is also found in Hereford. A spiral is associated with Essex and fans are associated with Wales.

The braiding and weaving techniques used to make corn dollies can be used to make all sorts of decorative objects for the home. The corn dollies in themselves are decorative but they can be combined to make mobiles, or stars can be made for seasonal decorations. Children as well as grown-ups will enjoy making them.

The straw most commonly used to make corn dollies is wheat. The straw should have a hollow center. Oats, rye barley and corn can also be used.

Cut the wheat when it is nearly ripe as it will give a longer length with which to work. The wheat is cut just above the first joint or node and usually below the ear to remove the sheath. Do not remove all the ears as they are used as well. Keep the wheat with the more attractive ears whole and try to select them in similar sizes.

Fertilizer tends to make the wheat brittle so try to find wheat which has been grown with a minimum amount of fertilizer.

Cutting the wheat can be a problem as the modern combine harvester threshes and generally mangles the wheat, separating the grain, which makes it unsuitable. Cutting by hand is best but it can be tiresome if you want a great deal. A tractor driven binder will provide suitable wheat as it cuts cleanly and ties the sheaves without too much damages to the ears.

Dry the straw by spreading it out on racks in the sun but if this is not possible bundles can be hung from rafters in a dry place or placed in a dry basement or in a slow oven with the door open. Once dry, straw can be stored for years.

Grade the straw before you work with

Red ribbons, symbolizing warmth, are tied to the Welsh fan to complete it. Made by Carolyn Tidmarsh.

it. Sort it out into two or three groups so that you have small and medium or large sizes. Compare the thickness of the wheat where it has been cut and the length of the stems and arrange them accordingly.

Storage must be in a dry atmosphere to prevent the straw from going moldy. Other hazards are mice, rats and seed eating birds like sparrows—they can do a lot of damage in a very short space of time.

Working with straw

Damping. Once the straw has been dried it will split if it is braided. To prevent this the straw must be soaked in water. The time taken to soften the wheat varies—depending on how dry it is. Test the wheat by pinching it, if it does not split it is ready to use. Do not oversoak the wheat as it becomes too soft to handle with ease.

Warm water will speed up the damping

A straw 'scythe'—a variation on a traditional corn dolly technique.

process. Do not let the ears get wet. Arrange a damp towel around the wheat while you are working—this prevents it from drying before you are ready to use it.

Paper straws

Getting hold of straw is not always easy as it is seasonal but if you stock up on it you will have plenty to keep you busy. If you are unable to obtain corn you can always use paper straws. Paper straws, similar to drinking straws, can be used in the same way as straw—the same techniques apply—but they do not require damping. The paper straws can be colored to improve their appearance.

In the next two chapters the techniques involved in working with straw are explained.

Ceramic and silver jewelry

The necklace

The necklace entails some ceramic work in making the serpent head and body which is formed by the beads. In the place of fired ceramic beads a self-hardening clay, available at most craft shops can be used. Alternatively, for the beads, three sizes of wooden doweling can be used. The doweling is cut into narrow disks and holes are then drilled through the center of each. These can be either painted or stained in a suitable color. The completed necklace is about 50cm (20″) long and is fastened with a silver wire hook.

You will need:

36cm (14″) of 1.2mm (16-18 gauge) thick silver wire.

107cm (42″) of 1.6mm (14-16 gauge) thick silver wire.

30cm (12″) of silver tubing 3mm (⅛″) in diameter.

6.5cm x 4cm (2½″ x 1½″) of .9mm (19-20 gauge) thick sheet silver.

Bottom left: a combination of ceramic and silver used successfully in this necklace designed by Pat de Menezes.

Once the finer points of silver soldering have been mastered, you can embark upon more intricate jewelry pieces. As seen in the previous metal chapter, other materials, such as ceramic or glass, can be combined with the silver to embellish the design of the jewelry. The necklace shown here illustrates the successful combination of materials to enrich the design and also shows how the use of jewelry can be extended beyond that of simple adornment.

The composition of the necklace; a clay serpent encircling the central motif of a woman's head, the fish, the apples, stars, the moon and suns, symbolize the Biblical story of Eve and the serpent and the notion of original sin. Thus, through symbolism, an alluring design has been given an added dimension.

This use of jewelry to incorporate cultural traditions is as old as the craft itself. Jewelry today, however, has come to be seen solely as ornamentation. In the past it was also an artistic embodiment of the beliefs upheld by those who made and wore the jewelry. By thinking in terms of modern cultural viewpoints as well as traditional ones, a wealth of new ideas and objects for jewelry design become available.

Jil Paul

Materials.

Stoneware clay or self-hardening clay for serpent head and beads.

Copper oxide powder to mix with clay.

Various thicknesses of wooden doweling—optional.

Toothpicks and cellophane tape.

Steel knitting needles, No.7 and No.5.

Steel and charcoal blocks.

Medium and soft silver solder.

Borax flux and saucer or flux tray in which to mix flux.

Fine paintbrush and teaspoon.

Pickle solution—either a solution of sulfuric acid or alum.

Glass dish for acid pickle and a pair of brass tongs.

Pumice powder, steel wool, soap, bicarbonate of soda, silver polish and an old toothbrush.

Nylon fishing line for stringing.

Metal drill or punch.

Other tools as for previous metal chapters.

Below: detail of the head of the necklace. Alongside is very similar jewelry made using the same shaping techniques.

Links

☐ Use a piercing or key hole saw to cut 115 links just under 2mm ($\frac{1}{16}''$) wide from tubing. If the links are too thick you will not have enough tubing—in which case use fewer links between beads when assembling.

☐ With a hand drill fastened in the vise and the No.7 knitting needle in the drill, make 15 large links from the .7mm (21-22 gauge) thick wire (see Metal chapter 29, page 2070).

☐ Repeat the procedure to make 24 medium-sized silver links on the No.5 needle, using the .45mm (25-26 gauge) thick silver wire.

☐ Then make five small links from the .45mm (25-26 gauge) thick wire. These links are made by twisting the wire around the end of the round-nosed pliers (see Metal chapter 1, page 24). You should now have 44 silver wire links and 115 silver tubing links. Prepare solution in which to clean the silver after soldering. This can be either a mixture of alum and water (Metal chapter 26, page 1874) or a dilute solution of sulfuric acid and water (Metal chapter 25, page 1841).

Charms

The necklace incorporates six silver charms. These are delicate pieces to solder so work carefully.

The size of the charms is a matter of choice, but they should be fairly delicate—no longer than 12mm ($\frac{1}{2}''$). If you do decide to alter the size of any part of the necklace, remember to keep in mind the overall proportions of the necklace and alter them accordingly.

Disk and link (fig.1). Cut three pieces of .7mm (21-22 gauge) thick wire, each 12mm ($\frac{1}{2}''$) long.

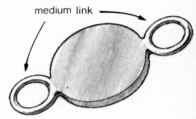

medium link

1. *Links soldered to disk to form charm.*

☐ Using a teaspoon, hollow out a shallow depression in the charcoal block about 12mm ($\frac{1}{2}''$) in diameter. This serves as a crucible in which to melt the silver.

☐ Place one piece of silver over the depression.

☐ Heat with a blowtorch until it melts and rolls up into a little ball.

☐ Repeat with the two remaining pieces of silver.

☐ Drop each ball into the cleaning solution, remove with brass tongs, and wash in a solution of bicarbonate of soda and water, then soap and water. Place to one side and allow to dry.

☐ Place each ball in turn on a steel block and hammer into a disk.

☐ Using medium silver solder, solder two medium-sized links on each side of the disks (see fig.1), and hammer flat.

Stars. To make these draw two triangles on a sheet of paper as shown in fig.2a. The sides of the triangles should be about 6mm ($\frac{1}{4}''$) long, though you may vary the size to suit yourself.

☐ Cut out the paper star and stick this to the sheet silver. Cut around the template with the saw.

☐ Make two stars. Using medium solder, fix a medium-sized link to each (fig.2b). Hammer links flat.

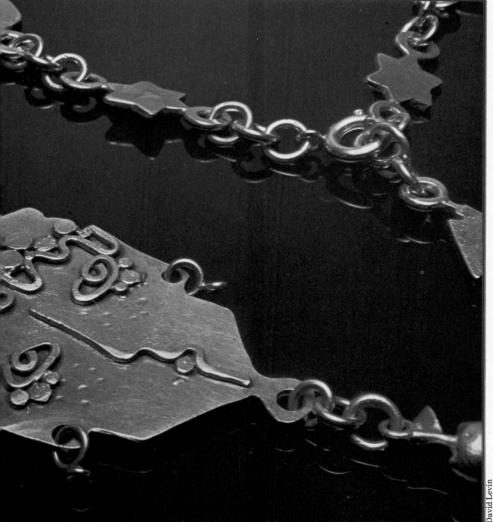

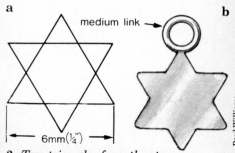

a

b

medium link

6mm($\frac{1}{4}''$)

2. *Two triangles form the star.*

David Levin

Paul Williams

Crescent moon. Make a paper template of a crescent-shaped moon, stick it to the sheet silver and cut out.
☐ Solder a medium-sized link to the top using medium solder.
Apples. Cut a piece of .7mm (21-22 gauge) thick silver wire 25mm (1") long.
☐ Bend the wire in half and place over the depression in the charcoal block.
☐ Heat with the blowtorch until the silver melts and forms a ball.
☐ Make two balls using this method.
☐ Place both balls in cleaning solution, then clean as for the disks.
☐ Using metal needle files carefully shape the top and bottom of the balls to resemble apples.
☐ Cut a piece of the .45mm (25-26 gauge) thick wire, 3mm (⅛") long and solder it to the apple to form the stem using medium solder.
☐ Cut out a small leaf and solder to the stem. Solder a small link above the leaf to the stem (fig.3) at the same time. Use soft solder.
☐ Repeat the procedure for the other apple.
Fish (fig.4a). This is cut from sheet silver as is the decoration for its head. The scales are made from three of the small links and the eye is made from a small bit of the silver wire (fig.4b).
☐ Solder the surface decoration to the fish using medium silver solder and, with soft solder, attach a medium link to each end (see fig. 4a).
Top knot charm. Cut a piece of .7mm (21-22 gauge) wire, 25mm (1") long and melt as for the apples.
☐ Open the ends of one of the large links and solder it to the ball (fig.5a).
☐ Place in a cleaning solution, dry and hammer the charm and link flat on the steel block (fig.5b).

Silver head

The silver head (fig.6a) forms the focal point of the necklace. It is cut from sheet silver and the features are cut from the thin wire.
☐ Trace the pattern for the head (see fig.6a) onto a piece of paper and cut out.
☐ Stick the paper template to the sheet silver with cellophane tape and cut out using the key hole saw.
☐ Use round-nosed and flat-nosed pliers to make the features and hair from .45mm (25-26 gauge) silver wire.
☐ Small silver balls are made by melting narrow sections cut from the silver tubing. These are then hammered flat and used as part of the hair decoration. All the features must be hammered flat carefully before soldering.
To solder the features, the head must be positioned so that the blowtorch can heat the head from underneath. The easiest way to do this is to place the head, face upwards across two

3. *Apple charm.*

4a, b. *Construction for the fish charm.*

5a. *Link soldered to ball.*
5b. *Charm hammered flat.*

6a. *Pattern for head.*

6b. *Heat underneath head to fix features.*

charcoal blocks or other suitable flame-proof material (fig.6b).
☐ Place the features upside down on the asbestos mat and melt soft solder onto the backs of them all.
☐ Place in cleaning solution, wash in soapy water and dry.
☐ Grind a thin solution of flux in a saucer or flux tray.
☐ Using fine tweezers, dip the back of each feature piece into the flux and place in position on the head.
☐ Heat the underside of the head. This causes the soft solder to melt, thus fastening the features.
☐ Place the head in cleaning solution and then wash and dry.

Ear-rings. These are for the silver head. Cut two pieces of .7mm (21-22 gauge) wire, 25mm (1") long and melt separately in a charcoal block to make two balls.
☐ Cut two 6mm (¼") long pieces of .45mm (25-26 gauge) wire.
☐ Solder a silver ball to one end of each of these lengths.
☐ To attach the ear-rings, drill or punch a hole through each ear-lobe. Pass the silver wire of the ear-ring through the hole and bend it with pliers.
☐ Punch or drill a hole at the top and bottom of the head. Smooth the rough edges of the hole with a metal file.

Serpent head and beads

The serpent head and beads which form its body are made from stoneware clay which is glazed and fired. A self-hardening clay can be used if you do not have a kiln in which to fire clay. Copper oxide is mixed with the clay to give it a rich, brown color.

The Serpent head. Mix the copper oxide with the clay until it is the right color.

☐ Roll a piece of clay into a ball about 19mm ($\frac{3}{4}$") in diameter.

☐ Flatten the ball slightly and shape it into a wedge (fig.7). This is the head of the serpent.

☐ Take another piece of clay and roll it into a cylindrical shape, 10mm ($\frac{3}{8}$") long and 3mm ($\frac{1}{8}$") in diameter.

☐ At each end of this shape make a small hole for the eyes. Use a toothpick to do this.

☐ Shape a half disk from the clay, 10mm ($\frac{3}{8}$") in diameter and 5mm ($\frac{3}{16}$") wide. This is the nose of the snake (see fig.7).

☐ Attach the eye and nose to the top of the head as shown in fig.8.

☐ Make a mouth by pressing a wooden toothpick sideways into the narrow end of the wedge (see fig.8). Be careful not to distort the shape of the head.

☐ Then, press the point of the toothpick through the center of the mouth and out through the back of the head. Twist the toothpick as you do, so that

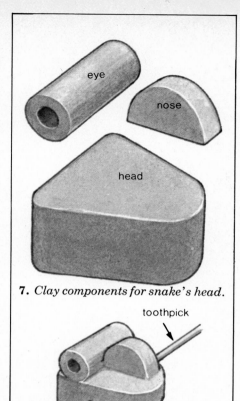

7. *Clay components for snake's head.*

8. *Use a toothpick to make mouth.*

it bores a clear tunnel through the clay.

The beads. There are 48 beads which make up the body of the snake. The beads are graded in size so that they become smaller toward the tail of the serpent.

☐ Roll up a small piece of clay into a ball. Press the ball flat, then press the toothpick down through the center.

☐ Twist the toothpick out of the clay, turn the disk over and, holding the disk in your hand, twist the toothpick through from the other side to complete the hole. This way you will not distort the bead.

☐ Fire the clay at 1250°C (2282°F) in a ceramic kiln if you have not used a self-hardening clay.

Alternatively, doweling can be used. This is cut into pieces and shaped with a wood file.

Polishing. String all the silver pieces onto a length of nylon fishing line. Use either a toothbrush and pumice powder or steel wool and soap to clean the silver. Use a soft cloth to give it a final polish.

Assembly

The necklace is assembled as shown in fig.9. Bend a short length of wire at one end, insert through serpent head and solder a loop to the other end. Make a hook for securing necklace and attach at tail end of serpent.

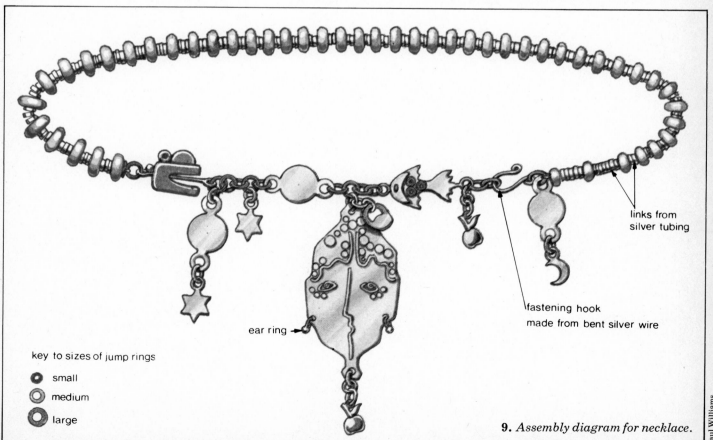

links from silver tubing

fastening hook made from bent silver wire

ear ring

key to sizes of jump rings

● small

◉ medium

◎ large

9. *Assembly diagram for necklace.*

Paul Williams

Water-based paints

Many different types of water-based paints are available from art stores. All have particular qualities which make them suitable for specific purposes.

Watercolors. These are translucent water-based paints specially made for watercolor painting which involves building up layers of translucent paint. Watercolors should be used thinly— very little paint is necessary to tint the water to the desired color—and the paper should always be visible through the paint.

The paint is available in tubes, in which case a little is squeezed onto a palette and mixed with water. It is also available in hard cakes, in which case a wet brush is brushed onto the cake and mixed with more water on the palette. It is better to buy the tubes if you want to use a lot of paint; and the cakes if you are using very little. The cakes are more convenient for using out of doors. They can be bought separately or in boxes and each individual cake can be replaced as it runs out.

Watercolor painting is a technique which takes a lot of practice—you cannot simply paint over your mistakes as you can when using opaque paint. If you are interested in this technique, many books are available on the subject from art and book stores.

Gouache. This is the best type of opaque water-based paint and is used by designers and in commercial art studios as well as for artistic painting. It comes in tubes and is mixed with water. It is a very smooth creamy paint which can be used quite thinly without losing its opacity. One color can be painted over another without the color underneath showing through, but if too many layers build up, the paint may crack off. This can be avoided by mixing a little gum arabic (also available from art stores) with the paint to make it more flexible and less likely to crack.

Gouache dries to a very smooth, slightly silky finish.

Poster paint is a cheaper opaque watercolor that can be used in the same way as gouache but will not give such a good finish. It comes in small jars or hard cakes and when dry it is completely flat.

It is possible to buy a water-based poster paint which is waterproof when dry. This is useful for paintings that may be exposed to rain or a humid atmosphere. Fluorescent, gold and silver poster paints are also available.

Powder paint is cheap but good for painting large areas of bold color. The powder is mixed with water—more or less water depending on the consistency desired. Large quantities of powder paint can easily be mixed in jam jars.

Powder paint is very popular in schools. It can also be used for tinting distemper and emulsion paint for such things as scenery painting.

Emulsion paint is a water-based paint used normally in interior decoration but also useful for painting any craft object. It can be used on most surfaces, but absorbent surfaces such as bare wood must first be sealed with a primer. While still wet, emulsion paint can be washed off with water, but once it has dried it is completely waterproof. So wash brushes immediately after use.

Emulsion paint comes in a wide variety of colors and is sold in hardware and home decorating stores as well as most large department stores.

Polymer color is made from acrylic polymer resin which can be dissolved with water when wet, but once dry is completely waterproof. It comes in tubes and can be used straight or mixed with special acrylic mediums.

Some acrylic mediums make the paint more liquid; other mediums will maintain the thick consistency of the paint so that it can be used in a similar way to oil paint. Water can be used in conjunction with any of these mediums to make a mixture more fluid.

It is also possible to add sand to polymer color for a textured effect. The painting technique used with polymer color will vary according to the medium used and the resulting consistency of paint.

Because this paint is waterproof when dry it is necessary to mix brushes and palettes in water immediately after use. If brushes do dry out they can be cleaned with a paint solvent or with hot water.

Acrylic mediums. Water-based paint is normally mixed with water which renders it runny and therefore restricts the painting techniques that can be employed. It is now possible to buy an acrylic of polymer medium which is mixed with water-based paint to make a very thick, jelly-like paint which enables different painting techniques to be used.

This medium can be used with any type of water-based paint mentioned earlier —powder paint should be mixed into a smooth paste before adding the medium. This acrylic medium is also a very strong latex glue and can be used for such things as collage.

Permanence. Some pigments are more permanent than others. If you want the colors in a design to last you must know which ones to use.

Most art suppliers have leaflets giving information on the permanence of each color. These leaflets will also give information on such things as opacity and which colors can successfully be painted over other colors.

Paul Kemp

AFTS CRAFTS CRAFTS CR
CRAFTS CRAFTS CRAFTS
AFTS CRAFTS CRAFTS CR
CRAFTS CRAFTS CRAFTS
AFTS CRAFTS CRAFTS CR
CRAFTS CRAFTS CRAFTS
AFTS CRAFTS CRAFTS CR
CRAFTS CRAFTS CRAFTS
AFTS CRAFTS CRAFTS CR
CRAFTS CRAFTS CRAFTS
AFTS CRAFTS CRAFTS CR
CRAFTS CRAFTS CRAFTS
AFTS CRAFTS CRAFTS CR
CRAFTS CRAFTS CRAFTS
AFTS CRAFTS CRAFTS CR
CRAFTS CRAFTS CRAFTS
AFTS CRAFTS CRAFTS CR
CRAFTS CRAFTS CRAFTS
AFTS CRAFTS CRAFTS CR